MATTHEW K

Prompt Engineering for Beginners

Master AI, Prompt Engineering, ChatGPT, Claude, and More to Work Smarter and Earn Faster

First edition

This book was professionally typeset on Reedsy.
Find out more at reedsy.com

Contents

Introduction

Ever wondered how some people manage to work less but earn more? Or how they can get machines to do the heavy lifting while they reap the rewards? In our rapidly evolving AI-driven world, this is not just possible—it's happening right now. Picture this: a small business owner uses AI to handle customer inquiries, freeing up hours to focus on growing their business. Or a freelancer who leverages AI tools to complete projects faster, leaving more time for other pursuits. This is the transformative power of prompt engineering, and it's waiting for you to tap into.

The purpose of this book is simple yet powerful. It aims to equip you with the knowledge and skills to thrive in the AI era. You'll learn the ins and outs of prompt engineering, using tools like ChatGPT and Claude to work smarter and earn faster. This isn't just about learning new technology; it's about unlocking new opportunities. Whether you're looking to start a new career, boost your current role, or just make some extra cash on the side, this book is your guide.

Let's talk about what you'll find in these pages. We'll start with the basics—what prompt engineering is and why it matters. From there, we'll dive into practical applications. You'll discover how to create effective prompts, work with AI tools, and explore real-world examples. As we progress, we'll cover advanced strategies and monetization techniques. Each chapter builds on the last, creating a solid foundation that will take you from beginner to confident practitioner.

This book is for you if you're a beginner in AI and prompt engineering. It's also for anyone looking to pivot into a new field or enhance their current career. No prior technical knowledge is required. Think of it as a friendly guide that's accessible to all, whether you're a curious novice or a seasoned professional ready to explore new avenues.

What sets this book apart? It's all about hands-on learning and real-world applications. You won't just read about prompt engineering—you'll do it. Plus, you'll gain access to exclusive resources and an online community. Here, you can connect with others on the same journey, share insights, and continue learning long after you've finished reading.

Now, a bit about me. I'm passionate about helping beginners navigate the exciting world of AI. I've spent years working in this field, mastering prompt engineering, and understanding how it can transform lives. My experience and insights are distilled into this book, offering you a trusted source to guide you every step of the way.

As you read, you can expect to gain valuable skills and knowledge. You'll learn how to apply prompt engineering in practical ways and explore monetization opportunities. By the end of this book, you'll be equipped to leverage AI tools to your advantage, opening doors to new possibilities.

Let me leave you with this thought: mastering prompt engineering isn't just about technology. It's about changing how you work and live. It's about freeing up time and creating new opportunities. I invite you to embark on this journey with me. Discover the potential that lies within AI and prompt engineering. Together, we'll explore the exciting landscape of possibilities waiting for you. Welcome to a smarter, more efficient way of working. Your adventure begins now.

1

Chapter 1: Foundations of AI and Prompt Engineering

Let's embark on a journey into the captivating realm of artificial intelligence, a technological marvel that's reshaping our world in profound ways. Picture yourself on a bustling morning. Your smartphone in hand becomes your indispensable ally. With a simple voice command, Siri sets your reminders—ensuring you won't miss that crucial meeting later in the day. Google Assistant effortlessly locates the closest café for a quick caffeine fix, while a virtual assistant helps orchestrate your chaotic schedule into something manageable. This harmonious integration of sophisticated technology into our everyday lives is the wonder of AI at work, and vividly represents just the beginning of its vast potential.

Understanding Artificial Intelligence: Simplified Concepts

Artificial Intelligence (AI), while often shrouded in mystery, can be broken down into fundamental ideas that are surprisingly approachable. At its core, AI aims to replicate human abilities like problem-solving and decision-making through advanced computing systems. Think of it as your tireless digital assistant—one that not only learns but also refines its processes over time. AI efficiently processes and synthesizes vast amounts of information, discerning patterns, and executing decisions based on the data it encounters. While the goal is not to fabricate machines that emulate human thought, it is about designing systems that elevate our human experience by taking on a variety of tasks we encounter daily.

Take for instance the manifestation of AI in our personal devices. When you command Siri or Google Assistant to perform a task, you're interacting with AI designed to interpret and understand the nuances of your speech. These AI-driven virtual assistants represent cutting-edge technology that parses our spoken words, gauges context, and delivers responses that feel as though they came from a human being. Such capabilities illustrate how AI facilitates smoother and more intuitive interactions, efficiently tackling routine matters.

The primary ambitions of AI are varied and transformative. One essential objective is the automation of repetitious tasks. By relieving us of these mundane chores, AI liberates our time, allowing us to engage in complex and creative pursuits. AI also enhances our decision-making processes by providing insights derived from analytics of extensive datasets. Imagine a realm where intricate data analysis transpires at lightning speed, providing solutions and forecasts that are beyond the reach of manual computation. In the realm of customer service, AI chatbots respond to inquiries with a swiftness and ease previously unimaginable, revolutionizing interactions and heightening operational efficiency.

The social impact of AI is significant and wide-reaching. Consider healthcare, where AI is revolutionizing diagnostics by meticulously examining medical data in record time. It unveils patterns that might escape even the most vigilant human experts, facilitating the earlier detection of diseases and enhancing patient outcomes. In logistics and supply chain management, AI streamlines processes by foreseeing demand trends and optimizing inventory management with precision. These progressive advancements showcase AI's pivotal role in fostering innovation and operational efficiency across diverse sectors.

Notwithstanding the myriad benefits of AI, certain myths and misconceptions persist. A common apprehension is the belief that AI will render human jobs obsolete. While it's true that AI automates certain functions, it concurrently cultivates new opportunities and transforms the job landscape, emphasizing roles that require advanced skill sets. Another fallacy is the notion of AI achieving consciousness or sentience. Despite its prowess, AI operates strictly within the confines of its programming; it lacks self-awareness or emotional capacity. Hence, it's vital to regard AI as a tool: incredibly potent yet ultimately restricted by its designed parameters.

Reflection Exercise

To deepen your comprehension of AI, reflect on its impact in your own life. Contemplate the devices and services you rely on daily. How do these applications harness AI to enhance your experience? Jot down three specific examples and consider how they have redefined your routines, leading to a seamless and more efficient daily existence.

Familiarizing yourself with these foundational principles of AI equips you to navigate the complex landscape of prompt engineering and related disciplines. Recall that AI is not here to supplant human abilities but to augment them. As you continue through this book, you will uncover how prompt engineering is central to unlocking AI's full potential, allowing you to strategically work more efficiently and thrive in the accelerating digital age.

The Role of Prompts in AI: A Beginner's Guide

In our exploration of artificial intelligence, prompts serve as the linchpin for effective interaction. To put it simply, a prompt is an instruction or input you provide to an AI system to generate a specific response. Imagine engaging in a conversation with a friend. You ask questions or share information, guiding the flow of dialogue. Similarly, prompts guide AI, shaping the direction and nature of its responses. Picture yourself using ChatGPT to whip up a dinner recipe. By typing "Give me a recipe for a vegetarian lasagna," you instruct the AI to compile a list of ingredients and steps—a digital sous-chef ready to assist.

The significance of well-crafted prompts cannot be overstated. They are vital for extracting useful and relevant output from AI. Consider the scenario of a business handling customer inquiries. By developing precise prompts, the AI can efficiently address common questions, providing timely and accurate responses that enhance customer satisfaction. A case study highlights how a company improved its customer service by refining prompts used in their chatbot system, which resulted in quicker resolution times and happier customers. Thus, the quality of AI output is directly tied to the clarity and specificity of the input prompts.

Crafting effective prompts requires some finesse but is within anyone's reach with a bit of practice. One fundamental strategy is using clear and direct language, much like giving instructions to a GPS. Ambiguity leads to confusion; hence, avoid vague prompts which leave room for interpretation. For example, instead of asking, "Tell me about lasagna," specify your needs with, "List the ingredients for a vegetarian lasagna recipe." This approach narrows down the possibilities, ensuring the AI aligns its response with your expectations.

The scope of prompt engineering extends across various domains, revolutionizing how we interact with technology. In content creation, for instance, AI can assist writers by generating article drafts or brainstorming ideas, all driven by specific prompts. This not only accelerates the writing process but also opens avenues for creativity and experimentation. Educational tools also benefit from prompt engineering. By tailoring prompts to student needs, AI-powered learning platforms provide personalized educational experiences that adapt to different learning styles and paces.

Prompt engineering is a game-changer in numerous fields, streamlining processes and enhancing productivity. In marketing, prompts guide AI to generate targeted ad copy that resonates with specific audiences. In healthcare, they assist in analyzing patient data to suggest personalized treatment options. The adaptability and versatility of prompt engineering allow it to be applied in ways that fundamentally transform how industries operate.

Exercise: Crafting Your Own Prompts

Try creating your own prompts to understand their impact. Choose a task you want an AI to help with—perhaps drafting an email or summarizing an article—and write two versions of a prompt: one vague and one detailed. Compare the AI's responses and note the differences in quality and relevance.

Understanding and applying prompt engineering opens doors to countless opportunities. It empowers individuals to communicate effectively with AI systems, ensuring they produce valuable and contextually appropriate outputs. As you develop your skills, remember that precision in your prompts is key—like tuning an instrument to achieve the perfect note. With practice, you will find that crafting prompts becomes second nature, allowing you to fully leverage the capabilities of AI systems like ChatGPT and Claude in your personal and professional endeavors.

Key Terms and Definitions in AI: Breaking Down the Jargon

Artificial intelligence can feel like a dense forest of jargon, but understanding the key terms can clear a path to clarity. Let's start with "machine learning." At its core, machine learning is about teaching computers to learn from data without explicit programming. Imagine teaching a child to recognize animals by showing them pictures. Over time, they begin to identify new animals they've never seen before. Similarly, machine learning algorithms sift through vast datasets, identifying patterns and making predictions based on the data they process. This capability is what powers everything from predictive text on your smartphone to complex financial forecasting models.

Next up, we have "algorithms." Think of an algorithm as a recipe for solving a problem. Just as you follow steps to bake a cake, an algorithm provides a step-by-step guide for computers to process information. Algorithms range from simple instructions to complex sequences that can sort through millions of data points in seconds. They form the backbone of AI, driving processes that include everything from sorting emails into folders to recommending your next favorite Netflix series.

Now, let's talk about "neural networks." These are inspired by the human brain and consist of layers of interconnected nodes, or "neurons," that process data. Picture a web of neurons in your brain firing to help you recognize a friend's face. Neural networks function similarly, used in tasks like image and speech recognition. They excel at handling tasks that require pattern recognition, such as identifying objects in images or translating languages in real-time.

AI systems also depend heavily on datasets, which are collections of information used to train models. Imagine datasets as the textbooks from which AI learns. They provide examples the AI uses to understand and learn patterns. For instance, a dataset of labeled images helps an AI system learn to differentiate between cats and dogs. The more diverse and comprehensive the dataset, the more effectively the AI can learn.

AI processes include training and validation. Training is akin to schooling, where the AI learns from examples provided in its dataset. The system adjusts its parameters based on input and output feedback, improving its predictions over time. Validation, on the other hand, assesses how well the AI has learned by testing it on new data. This step ensures the AI doesn't just memorize but generalizes its learning to new situations, much like a student applying classroom knowledge to real-world problems.

Connecting these terms back to practical applications can illuminate their relevance. Consider neural networks in action: when you upload a photo on social media and it automatically tags your friends, that's neural networks at work. Or think about algorithms in recommendation systems—whether it's suggesting a new book based on your reading history or new songs after you finish a playlist. These systems analyze your past behavior to predict what you might enjoy next, always learning and improving their suggestions.

These components together create AI systems that transform industries and redefine efficiency. In healthcare, for example, AI sifts through patient records using algorithms to identify potential health risks and recommend preventive measures. Retailers use machine learning to enhance supply chain logistics, predicting inventory needs with remarkable accuracy.

Understanding these terms is like having a key to unlock AI's full potential. With this knowledge, you'll find yourself more adept at navigating conversations about AI and recognizing its impact on your life and work. The language of AI isn't just for tech experts—it's for anyone who wants to grasp how this technology is shaping our world. As you continue reading, you'll see how these building blocks of AI come together in prompt engineering, enabling you to harness technology's power for smarter work and faster earnings.

Introduction to Natural Language Processing (NLP)

Natural Language Processing, or NLP, is the unsung hero behind the scenes that enables computers to understand, interpret, and respond to human language. It's the technology that makes it possible for machines to engage in conversations with us in ways that feel remarkably human. Imagine a translation app on a bustling city street. You speak into your phone in English, and it instantly relays your words in Spanish to the vendor across the stall. This seamless exchange is NLP in action, breaking down language barriers with ease. At its core, NLP is about bridging the gap between human communication and computer understanding.

The significance of NLP within AI cannot be overstated. It plays a pivotal role in our interactions with AI systems like ChatGPT. These systems rely on NLP to parse user inputs, grasp context, and generate coherent responses. Consider chatbots and virtual assistants—a domain where NLP shines brightly. When you ask a virtual assistant about the weather or request it to play your favorite song, NLP is at work behind the scenes, interpreting your requests and executing the appropriate actions. It's this capability that allows AI to comprehend and engage in meaningful dialogue with us.

NLP encompasses a range of techniques that enhance AI interactions. One such technique is sentiment analysis, which evaluates customer feedback by determining the emotional tone behind words. For instance, if a user leaves a review stating, "The service was outstanding, but the wait was too long," sentiment analysis helps identify mixed sentiments, providing businesses with valuable insights into customer satisfaction. Another technique is entity recognition, which identifies and categorizes key elements in text—such as names, dates, or locations—to streamline information retrieval and organization. These techniques collectively refine AI's ability to interpret and respond to human language with accuracy.

Despite its capabilities, NLP faces several challenges. One of the most significant is understanding context and linguistic nuances. Human language is replete with ambiguities; words can have multiple meanings depending on the context. Take the word "bank," for example. It could refer to a financial institution or the side of a river, depending on the conversation. NLP systems must discern these subtleties to provide relevant responses. Moreover, sarcasm and idiomatic expressions pose additional hurdles. A phrase like "Yeah, right" can convey skepticism rather than agreement, yet machines often struggle to capture this nuance.

To navigate these complexities, NLP systems employ advanced algorithms designed to detect patterns and contextual cues within language. However, despite these advancements, challenges persist. Understanding idiomatic expressions or deciphering sarcasm continues to test the boundaries of NLP capabilities. The beauty of human language lies in its richness and variability, attributes that machines still grapple with fully comprehending.

Reflecting on everyday interactions reveals the pervasive influence of NLP in our lives. When you use a voice-activated assistant to set reminders or navigate your route home, NLP is the driving force that makes these interactions seamless and intuitive. It's the technology that empowers us to communicate effortlessly with machines, opening new avenues for efficiency and innovation.

As we delve deeper into the world of AI and prompt engineering, appreciating the role of NLP becomes increasingly important. It's what makes AI not only functional but also relatable and engaging. Understanding this connection helps demystify AI systems like ChatGPT, which rely heavily on NLP to deliver precise responses tailored to our needs.

In exploring NLP further, consider its impact on industries like customer service, where chatbots utilize sentiment analysis to gauge customer satisfaction and tailor responses accordingly. Or in healthcare, where entity recognition aids in extracting critical patient information from clinical notes. These applications highlight the transformative potential of NLP across various domains.

By grasping the fundamentals of NLP and recognizing its challenges, you'll gain insight into how AI systems interpret language—an invaluable asset as you navigate the world of prompt engineering. As you continue to engage with AI technologies, keep in mind that NLP serves as the crucial link between human expression and machine comprehension, enabling meaningful interactions that drive progress in our digital age.

How AI Models Like ChatGPT and Claude Work

Stepping into the mechanics of AI models like ChatGPT and Claude reveals a fascinating blend of structure, sophistication, and strategy, a true testament to the marvels of modern technology. At the heart of these sophisticated systems lies an intricate architecture, comparable to a meticulously crafted recipe, which serves as a guiding framework, ensuring consistency and coherence in response generation. Visualize a master chef in a bustling kitchen, navigating through complex ingredients, yet following a well-refined recipe to deliver a consistent and remarkable dish every time without fail. Similarly, AI models are built upon a set of predefined protocols and structures—commonly referred to as neural networks. These networks encompass a plethora of interconnected nodes, or "neurons," that closely mimic the intricate synaptic connections found within the human brain. This neural architecture enables the model to analyze vast amounts of information and subsequently produce responses that are meaningful, coherent, and contextually appropriate.

The training procedure for these AI systems is akin to teaching a language through immersion in diverse and sprawling conversational environments. The process commences with the introduction of extensive datasets, rich with text sourced from a plethora of books, articles, websites, and other repositories of human knowledge, allowing the models to recognize patterns, establish relationships, and understand the nuances present in language. Feedback loops are pivotal within this context; they provide the indispensable mechanism for the models to refine their understanding, enhance their capabilities, and learn effectively from their mistakes. This iterative cycle ensures that the AI models grow progressively more adept at discerning context and generating responses accurately. It's comparable to coaching an athlete: with every rigorous practice session, the athlete polishes and hones their skills, becoming ever more dexterous and proficient in their sport.

Upon reaching completion of their training regimen, these models are poised to leap into action, ready and eager to address user queries with a degree of finesse and adeptness previously unimaginable. When a user types a question or command, the model embarks on an interpretive journey by deconstructing the input into "tokens," which are small units of data. This segmentation into tokens facilitates the model's ability to grasp the essence and underlying intent of what is being asked or communicated. It then taps into its expansive, learned knowledge base, routing these tokens through the labyrinthine layers of its neural network to predict and formulate the most pertinent and appropriate response. This intricate, yet lightning-fast sequence of orchestration between input and output transpires almost instantaneously, culminating in replies that exude a surprisingly human-like quality.

In practical, real-world scenarios, these AI models demonstrate their formidable prowess across a multitude of applications, each as consequential as the next. Take, for instance, ChatGPT within the realm of automated customer service; it serves as the initial touchpoint for customers in need of assistance, providing prompt and immediate answers to a wide gamut of common inquiries. This not only elevates customer satisfaction and enhances user experience but simultaneously liberates human agents, allowing them to allocate their time and efforts to more complex, nuanced issues that demand their specialized skills and attention. On the other hand, Claude finds its niche in content generation, aiding writers by crafting article drafts, generating creative ideas, or assisting in editing and proofreading. Through leveraging its robust ability to understand context and generate coherent text, Claude significantly empowers content creators, enabling them to streamline workflows and bolster productivity with remarkable efficiency.

Interactive Element: Delving into Case Studies

To enrich and deepen your understanding of these AI models' inner workings, consider exploring a comprehensive case study that focuses on ChatGPT's integral role in reshaping and revamping a company's customer service infrastructure. Analyze the ways in which the AI model has contributed to improving response times and elevating customer satisfaction, ultimately playing a pivotal role in boosting overall business efficiency and performance.

These AI models epitomize a powerful, seamless fusion of cutting-edge technology and nuanced language capabilities, offering expansive solutions that are as diverse as they are impactful. As you engage with these innovative systems, remember that their resounding success fundamentally hinges on their foundational architecture, rigorous and comprehensive training processes, and continuous refinement. By gaining insights into these complex, dynamic processes, you equip yourself with the valuable knowledge required to harness their extraordinary capabilities effectively, whether it be for personal exploration, academic inquiry, creative endeavors, or professional pursuits.

Demystifying Algorithms: A Non-Technical Overview

Algorithms are at the heart of AI, serving as its backbone by providing a clear set of instructions for how it operates. Think of an algorithm as similar to a recipe that guides you through the steps needed to bake a cake. Just as you would follow each step meticulously to achieve that perfect sponge, AI follows algorithms to solve specific problems. These step-by-step instructions ensure that the AI executes tasks consistently, whether it's sorting through data or making predictions. Algorithms are the building blocks that allow AI to function effectively, transforming complex data into actionable insights that drive decision-making processes across various applications.

In the diverse world of algorithms, there exists an array of types, each suited to particular tasks within AI. Sorting algorithms, for instance, are indispensable in organizing data. Imagine trying to alphabetize a list of names or arrange a collection of numbers from smallest to largest. Sorting algorithms streamline these tasks efficiently, enabling systems to manage and retrieve data with ease. Then there are search algorithms, which excel in information retrieval. These are akin to having a librarian who knows exactly where every book is located. When you search for something online, these algorithms sift through vast amounts of information to find exactly what you need in a fraction of a second. Together, these algorithms form the foundation of many AI systems, optimizing how they handle, process, and analyze data.

Algorithms do more than just organize and retrieve; they empower AI's decision-making capabilities. Take decision trees, for example. These algorithms are like flowcharts that guide AI through a series of choices based on data inputs. In predictive analytics, decision trees play a crucial role by helping systems evaluate potential outcomes and make informed decisions. Picture a health app predicting potential illness based on your symptoms and medical history—it uses decision trees to assess risks and suggest preventive measures. By breaking down complex decisions into manageable steps, algorithms enable AI to provide valuable insights and recommendations that are both precise and actionable.

Despite their utility, algorithms are not without challenges. One significant concern is bias, which can inadvertently creep into algorithms and skew results. Consider facial recognition technology; if an algorithm is trained predominantly on one demographic, it may struggle to recognize faces from other groups accurately. This bias can have serious implications in security and law enforcement applications. Therefore, designing ethical algorithms that account for diversity and inclusivity is paramount. AI developers must remain vigilant in evaluating and refining their models to ensure fairness and accuracy. This involves continuous monitoring and testing to detect and address any biases that may arise.

Ethical considerations extend beyond addressing bias. They encompass ensuring transparency in how algorithms function and make decisions. Users should have a basic understanding of how these systems operate, especially when they impact critical areas like healthcare or finance. Transparency builds trust and allows for accountability, ensuring that algorithms serve humanity's best interests. Additionally, as AI becomes more integrated into our lives, protecting privacy and maintaining data security are imperative considerations that cannot be overlooked.

In every application of AI, from enhancing customer experience to revolutionizing industries, algorithms play a pivotal role. They are the silent operators behind the scenes, driving efficiency and innovation by executing precise instructions with remarkable accuracy. As we continue to explore the vast possibilities of AI, understanding the importance of algorithms is key. Their ability to transform raw data into meaningful insights makes them indispensable tools in our quest for progress.

As we conclude this exploration of AI fundamentals, it's clear that the potential applications are as diverse as they are transformative. From simple tasks like organizing your digital photo album to complex operations such as predicting market trends, the possibilities with AI are truly expansive. By understanding these foundational concepts—prompts, NLP, AI models, and algorithms—you're now equipped with the knowledge to navigate this exciting landscape confidently. The world of AI beckons with opportunities waiting to be explored and harnessed for both personal and professional growth. Embrace this knowledge and let it guide you toward smarter work practices and innovative solutions in your everyday life.

2

Chapter 2: Crafting Effective Prompts

The Anatomy of a Successful Prompt

Imagine you're in a bustling café, trying to get the barista's attention during the morning rush. If you simply shout, "Coffee!" you're likely to get a confused look. But if you say, "A large black coffee with two sugars, please," you've crafted a prompt that's clear and specific. The same principle applies to AI. Crafting effective prompts is about ensuring clarity, specificity, and context to get you exactly what you want from AI systems like ChatGPT and Claude.

First, clarity in language is crucial. Avoid complex wording or tech jargon that could confuse the AI. Think of your prompt as a conversation with a friend who needs straightforward instructions. Using simple, direct language not only makes it easier for the AI to understand but also improves the accuracy of its responses. For instance, instead of asking, "Could you possibly elaborate on the intricacies of the financial report?" simplify it to, "Explain the financial report highlights."

Specificity in prompts ensures that the AI doesn't wander off course. When you provide precise instructions, you're setting clear boundaries within which the AI can operate. This could be as simple as saying, "Summarize the article in three bullet points," rather than just, "Summarize the article." By being specific, you're guiding the AI to focus its output, which is particularly useful when time or space is limited.

Context is another key player in crafting effective prompts. It's what transforms a simple request into a targeted command. Let's say you're scheduling a meeting. Including context like "Schedule the meeting for next Tuesday at 3 PM" ensures that the AI understands not just the task but also when and where to apply it. Contextual cues like these help the AI generate responses that are relevant and timely. According to a source on LinkedIn, providing detailed context leads to more relevant AI responses (The Importance of Context: Crafting Effective Prompts for Better AI Output).

Intent plays a pivotal role in how the AI interprets your prompt. Whether your goal is to inform or direct will shape how you phrase your request. If you're looking for information, your prompt might be exploratory, such as "What are the latest trends in renewable energy?" But if you're directing action, it should be instructive: "List three renewable energy sources to research." Being explicit about your intent helps the AI align its output with your expectations.

Striking a balance between length and detail is another aspect of effective prompt crafting. You don't want a prompt so brief that it lacks clarity nor one so verbose that it overwhelms. For example, if you're querying an AI about vacation spots, saying, "Suggest 3 beach destinations for a family trip" balances brevity with necessary detail. This ensures that the AI understands the context and provides a focused response without unnecessary fluff.

Exercise: Craft Your Own Prompt

Take a moment to think about a task you'd like an AI to assist with—perhaps planning a weekly meal menu or summarizing a lengthy document. Write two versions of this prompt: one with minimal detail and another with clarity and context included. Compare how each version might influence the AI's response.

Crafting successful prompts involves understanding these components and how they interact to shape outcomes. Whether it's simplicity in language or embedding context, each element plays its part in ensuring effective communication with AI. As you refine your prompts, you'll find greater consistency and accuracy in the responses you receive. This chapter sets the foundation for using AI tools to their fullest potential, opening up avenues for smarter work and innovative solutions tailored to your needs.

Step-by-Step Guide to Crafting Prompts

Crafting prompts is a bit like cooking a new dish. You start with an idea, mix in some ingredients, refine the flavors, and taste as you go. The process begins with brainstorming. Think about what you want the AI to achieve. Are you looking for a detailed analysis or a quick summary? Jot down ideas without worrying about perfection. This is your creative phase. Once you have a concept, move on to drafting. Here, structure is key. Organize your thoughts into a coherent prompt. Aim for clarity and completeness. Don't be afraid to draft several versions. Like a sculptor chiseling away at marble, each revision brings you closer to the final form.

Feedback is your secret weapon in refining prompts. Once your draft is ready, test it with the AI. Observe how it responds. Does it hit the mark or miss entirely? Use these results to tweak your wording. This is iterative testing—a cycle of trial and error that sharpens your prompt's effectiveness. Adjust phrases, reword sections, and try different angles. By doing so, you'll slowly hone in on a prompt that delivers consistently good results.

Let's look at examples to illustrate each step. Imagine you start with a basic prompt: "Tell me about climate change." The AI might provide a broad overview. Now, refine it: "Summarize the impact of climate change on polar ice caps in three bullet points." Notice how the refined version is focused and clear. It guides the AI to deliver specific information, showcasing how small adjustments can significantly improve outcomes.

Tools and techniques can further enhance your prompts. Online resources like grammar checkers ensure clarity and correctness, eliminating ambiguity that might confuse the AI. Websites such as Grammarly are invaluable for this purpose, offering insights into sentence structure and word choice.

Additionally, there are AI-specific tools designed for prompt engineering. These platforms offer templates and suggestions based on successful prompts from various domains, giving you a solid starting point for crafting your own.

Incorporating feedback loops into your workflow is crucial for continuous improvement. After each interaction with the AI, take note of what worked and what didn't. This process not only refines individual prompts but also sharpens your overall prompt crafting skills. Over time, you'll develop an intuitive sense for what makes an effective prompt.

Imagine using these techniques to draft a prompt for a virtual assistant tasked with scheduling meetings: "Arrange a meeting with John next Wednesday at 2 PM." Test this with the AI and examine its response. Did it confirm the meeting accurately? If not, adjust your wording: "Schedule a 30-minute meeting with John Smith for Wednesday, March 15th, starting at 2 PM Eastern Time." This version eliminates potential confusion by providing specific details.

The journey doesn't end with drafting and testing. Embrace the iterative nature of prompt engineering as a continuous cycle of learning and optimization. Think of each prompt as an opportunity to experiment and innovate. Explore different styles and formats. Perhaps you'll find that bullet points work better than paragraphs for certain tasks or that framing instructions as questions elicits more detailed responses.

In your quest to craft effective prompts, remember that practice makes perfect. Like learning any new skill, prompt engineering improves with experience and persistence. Embrace mistakes as learning opportunities rather than setbacks. Each misstep brings valuable insights that guide future success.

Prompts can be powerful tools when wielded effectively. They shape how AI systems understand and respond to our requests, ultimately influencing the quality of interactions we experience. By following a structured approach to prompt creation—brainstorming ideas, drafting with intention, incorporating feedback loops, and leveraging available tools—you'll unlock the full potential of AI technologies like ChatGPT and Claude.

Your toolkit now includes not just prompts but strategies for refining them into precise instruments of communication. You hold the reins of innovation in your hands, ready to explore new frontiers in AI interaction through meticulously crafted prompts that speak directly to your needs and aspirations.

Common Pitfalls in Prompt Creation and How to Avoid Them

Creating effective prompts can feel like walking a tightrope, where one wrong step could lead to a fall. Missteps often seem innocuous at first. Ambiguous language sits among the top offenders, leading the AI down a path of misinterpretation. When you ask an AI to "Tell me about events," it might start recounting historical timelines or list upcoming concerts, depending on its whim. The lack of specificity in language leaves too much room for interpretation, causing AI to stumble over its responses. To counter this, strive for precise language. Specify, "Detail major world events in 2023," and watch your AI hit the mark with pinpoint accuracy.

Bias is another sneaky culprit in prompt design. It's easy to unintentionally infuse your prompts with assumptions that skew AI outputs. For instance, asking, "Why do young people prefer social media over books?" assumes a preference that may not hold true universally. Such bias can distort the information the AI provides. To combat this, phrase your prompts neutrally: "What are common reasons people use social media more than reading books?" This way, you allow the AI to explore various angles without being led astray by preconceived notions.

Avoiding these pitfalls involves honing your skills and being aware of the impact of context sensitivity in prompts. Imagine you're programming an AI calendar assistant to set appointments. Without proper context, a prompt like "Schedule a meeting" could result in an AI setting up a 3 AM slot—technically accurate but practically useless. Context is crucial here; you should specify "Schedule a meeting with Emily on Tuesday afternoon." This ensures the AI aligns with your intent and your reality (The Importance of Context: Crafting Effective Prompts for Better AI Output).

Overly complex prompts present their own set of challenges. When faced with a tangled web of instructions, AI can flounder, leading to ineffective or convoluted responses. Think of asking someone to "Prepare a three-course meal with a chicken entrée, using ingredients sourced locally and seasonally while considering dietary restrictions for gluten and lactose." It's better to break it down: "Prepare a chicken entrée for a three-course meal using local, seasonal ingredients. Consider gluten and lactose restrictions." This approach simplifies tasks into manageable chunks, allowing AI to process each element effectively.

Complex ideas often need simplification for clarity. Consider breaking down intricate concepts into digestible parts, just like untangling a knot one strand at a time. When crafting prompts that tackle complex issues, ask yourself if there's a simpler way to convey the same message. This not only aids AI comprehension but also enhances the relevance and accuracy of its responses.

Striking the right balance between detail and simplicity is key to avoiding these common pitfalls. As you craft prompts, remember that clarity comes from precision and context, not verbosity or complexity. Keep your language clear and your intentions explicit. By doing so, you'll steer clear of ambiguity and bias while ensuring your prompts are as effective as possible.

Incorporating these strategies into your prompt design will help you sidestep errors that often trip up beginners. Whether you're scheduling meetings, generating creative content, or managing data analysis tasks, these principles will guide you toward more successful interactions with AI systems like ChatGPT and Claude.

As you become more adept at recognizing and avoiding these pitfalls, you'll find that your ability to craft precise, effective prompts will significantly improve. Your prompts will become tools for unlocking the full potential of AI technology, enabling you to leverage its capabilities in meaningful and innovative ways.

Case Studies: Successful Prompt Engineering in Action

Consider the case of an e-commerce company that integrated a chatbot into their customer service operations. The goal was to reduce response time and improve user satisfaction. Initially, the chatbot struggled with vague prompts, leaving customers frustrated. Here, specific and concise prompts made all the difference. By refining the prompt strategy, they tailored questions like, "Help me track my recent order," which provided clarity and context, allowing the AI to perform efficiently. This refinement led to a 30% increase in customer satisfaction scores and reduced churn rates, proving that well-crafted prompts can significantly impact business outcomes.

In educational technology, AI-driven platforms use prompts to guide student learning. One example involved an online tutoring system that initially asked, "Do you have any questions?" This open-ended prompt often left students unsure of how to engage. By tweaking it to, "What specific topic would you like to explore today?" the platform saw a 50% increase in student interaction. This change encouraged students to think about their learning goals actively. The iterative refinement of these prompts not only increased engagement but also helped students achieve better learning outcomes, demonstrating a clear win for personalized education through targeted prompting.

The strategies employed in these cases reveal a common thread: iterative refinement. By continuously testing and tweaking prompts based on user feedback, both companies managed to align AI responses with user expectations more closely. This process of refinement mirrors how writers revise drafts for clarity and impact. Each iteration brought them closer to optimal performance. Understanding what worked involved paying attention to user feedback and adapting prompt structures accordingly, allowing for better alignment with user needs over time. These strategies highlight the importance of flexibility and responsiveness in crafting prompts that truly resonate.

From these examples, we extract valuable lessons applicable across various domains. Successful prompts often share traits such as clarity, specificity, and relevance. They are concise yet rich in context, guiding AI toward delivering precise responses. Learning from cross-industry applications further enriches this insight. For instance, while the e-commerce chatbot focused on transactional prompts, the educational platform emphasized exploratory prompts. Both approaches highlight the versatility of prompt engineering across different fields, underscoring its adaptability and potential for innovation.

Prompts find diverse applications beyond e-commerce and education. In healthcare, they optimize patient interactions with AI systems. Consider an AI designed to assist doctors by analyzing patient symptoms: prompts like "List possible diagnoses for headaches" streamline diagnostic processes, improving efficiency. This application not only aids in faster decision-making but also enhances patient care by providing doctors with quick access to relevant information. Similarly, automated customer service benefits from strategic prompting. By asking specific questions like "Are you inquiring about billing or technical support?" AI systems can route users more effectively, reducing wait times and improving service quality.

These diverse applications demonstrate how prompt engineering adapts across industries and scenarios, enhancing efficiency and effectiveness. Whether it's guiding students toward academic success or helping businesses streamline operations, well-crafted prompts serve as powerful tools that bridge the gap between human intention and machine comprehension. They empower AI systems to deliver meaningful interactions tailored to users' needs, driving innovation across sectors.

By dissecting real-life examples of successful prompt engineering, we gain insight into the strategies that lead to effective outcomes. These case studies offer a glimpse into the transformative power of prompts when thoughtfully crafted and strategically employed. As you continue exploring prompt engineering's potential in your work or projects, remember that success often lies in the details—those small iterations that refine and perfect each interaction with AI.

Interactive Exercises: Practicing Prompt Crafting

Imagine you're handed a blank canvas and a palette filled with vibrant colors. Crafting prompts is much like painting, where your words are the brushstrokes that shape the AI's responses. To practice this, let's dive into some hands-on activities designed to sharpen your prompt-crafting skills. These exercises will help you explore the nuances of creating effective prompts while challenging you to apply them in various contexts.

Begin by envisioning a scenario: you're tasked with crafting prompts for a travel assistant AI. Your goal is to ensure travelers receive personalized recommendations for their next adventure. Start with a simple prompt like "Recommend a destination," then iterate by adding layers of detail: "Suggest a family-friendly beach destination in the Caribbean for December." This exercise encourages you to think about the elements of specificity and context, ensuring your prompts are both clear and targeted.

Next, switch gears to designing prompts for a virtual tutor. Picture a student struggling with algebra, seeking guidance from AI. Craft an initial prompt: "Help solve quadratic equations." Then refine it: "Explain the steps to solve quadratic equations with examples." By practicing this exercise, you'll learn how to guide the AI to provide comprehensive educational support, enhancing its ability to deliver clear and helpful responses.

Incorporating a variety of scenarios broadens your understanding of prompt applications. For instance, consider crafting engaging prompts for storytelling AI. Challenge yourself to create prompts that inspire creativity and innovation: "Generate a mystery plot set in Victorian London involving a secret society." This pushes you to experiment with different styles and genres, showcasing how prompts can be tailored to evoke vivid and imaginative responses from AI systems.

Providing immediate feedback and solutions is crucial for refining your skills. After crafting your prompts, compare them with sample solutions to identify areas for improvement. If you're working on travel recommendations, see how your prompts stack up against examples that incorporate traveler preferences or seasonal highlights. This feedback loop allows you to refine your approach and develop a keen sense of what makes an effective prompt.

Encourage creativity by experimenting with diverse prompt structures. Don't be afraid to think outside the box and try unconventional approaches. For example, when working on storytelling prompts, explore different narrative perspectives or incorporate unique plot twists. This experimentation not only hones your prompt-crafting abilities but also unleashes the full potential of AI, resulting in richer and more engaging interactions.

To provide feedback and solutions, reflect on the prompts you've crafted. Consider how well they achieved their intended purpose and what adjustments could enhance their effectiveness. Think of it as a self-assessment tool, guiding you toward continual improvement. By evaluating your prompts and comparing them with expert examples, you gain valuable insights into the elements that contribute to successful AI interactions.

In these exercises, aim for clarity without sacrificing creativity. Challenge yourself to create prompts that are both precise and innovative, allowing the AI to deliver meaningful responses while sparking curiosity. As you practice, remember that each prompt is an opportunity to refine your skills and explore new possibilities.

Through these interactive exercises, you're not just learning how to craft prompts; you're building a foundation for effective communication with AI systems. Whether you're designing prompts for travel recommendations or educational support, these activities equip you with the tools to engage AI in meaningful ways. As you continue practicing, you'll discover that crafting effective prompts is not just a skill—it's an art form that empowers you to unlock the full potential of AI technology.

Troubleshooting Ineffective Prompts

In the intricate and ever-evolving cosmos of prompt engineering, not every crafted prompt achieves its intended goal. Even with diligent preparation and ample knowledge, AI responses can occasionally stray wildly from the desired path—sometimes being irrelevant or, in the worst-case scenario, completely incorrect. Recognizing these symptoms is crucial, serving as the initial step towards enhancement and refinement. You might observe that the AI drifts off-topic, struggles to provide coherent or comprehensive information, or delivers answers that completely miss the essence of your query. These are the unmistakable signs of an ineffective prompt, highlighting the need for a closer examination of underlying issues.

Diagnosing the root causes of ineffective prompts requires more than a cursory glance; it demands a methodical and analytical approach akin to detective work. Most often, these issues originate from language ambiguity—instances where the prompt is not as clear, concise, or precise as it could be, leading to confused or muddled AI interpretations. Imagine a scenario where you are stepping into the AI's shoes. Ask yourself: Is the language explicit and unambiguous? Are there multiple interpretations of what is being asked that could potentially lead to confusion? Does the prompt provide enough context for the AI to fully comprehend the task at hand? By delving into these aspects, you can pinpoint exactly where things might be going awry, illuminating the path toward resolution.

Once you've identified potential problem areas, it's time to formulate and implement strategic solutions. Begin by rephrasing the problematic prompt. Break down complex language into simpler terms and ensure your questions are straightforward and devoid of ambiguity. If an AI persistently returns irrelevant data, experiment with different phrasings and incorporate precise keywords that can focus its attention effectively. This method of systematically testing variations can elucidate which adjustments lead to more accurate and refined results. This iterative and trial-and-error method is invaluable, enabling you to hone and refine prompts until they consistently achieve their intended objectives.

Consistent evaluation is an integral component in ensuring the effectiveness and accuracy of prompts over time. Crafting a good prompt is not a one-time task but a continuous journey; ongoing review and optimization are essential to sustain and enhance performance. AI systems evolve, as do user needs and contexts, making it crucial to periodically revisit and reassess your prompts to ensure they remain relevant and effective. Consider establishing a regular schedule for evaluating your prompts, examining their performance over time, and making necessary adjustments. This relentless and ongoing process ensures that your interactions with AI remain sharp, responsive, and perfectly aligned with both current demands and the trends of the future.

Continuous refinement is not solely about rectifying inefficiencies. It also represents a golden opportunity to innovate and incrementally enhance the quality of your prompts over time. Engage with feedback loops by systematically collecting insights from AI responses and utilizing them to inform and guide future iterations. This dynamic and fluid cycle of evaluation and adjustment fosters an environment where creativity and functionality complement each other, driving substantial improvements in how AI understands and responds to human prompts.

The capacity to troubleshoot effectively is an indispensable skill for anyone immersed in the world of AI prompts. It equips you with the ability to transform common stumbling blocks into stepping stones for more sophisticated interactions with technology. By recognizing symptoms of ineffective prompts, diagnosing underlying issues, implementing strategic solutions, and maintaining a consistent evaluation routine, you position yourself to fully harness AI's vast capabilities in ways that are both efficient and deeply rewarding.

As we bring this chapter on crafting prompts to a close, it is important to remember that each prompt represents a conversation starter with AI—a bridge linking human intent with the vast and varied capabilities of the machine. The insights and knowledge gained here lay a firm foundation for more complex applications and interactions that are yet to come. In the forthcoming chapter, we will explore how these foundational skills seamlessly translate into real-world scenarios where AI can significantly augment productivity and innovation across diverse sectors. Whether you are streamlining business operations or enhancing educational experiences, well-crafted and carefully considered prompts are your key to unlocking AI's full and remarkable potential.

3

Chapter 3: Real-World Applications of Prompt Engineering

Prompt Engineering in Customer Service and Support

Picture this scenario: you've just eagerly unwrapped a new gadget delivered to your doorstep after a much-anticipated wait. Inside the box, the sleek design sparkles, the promise of new technology awaiting your interaction. However, there's a challenge—an intricate setup process greets you, perplexing in its complexity. Frustration bubbles up almost immediately, and the impulse to seek assistance is undeniable. Enter prompt engineering, an innovative solution crafted to meet such needs with precision and flair, acting as a seamless bridge between confusion and clarity in customer service.

At the forefront of this technological interaction are chatbots, ever-present, ever-ready, patiently waiting to assist with your queries. These digital aides, operating around the clock, leverage the power of carefully devised prompts to steer and refine interactions. Through this intelligent system, support becomes not only efficient but strikingly satisfying. For instance, when a customer inputs "How do I set up my device?" into a chat window, this seemingly simple query initiates a sophisticated sequence. Untapped potential bursts to life as AI, fortified by a robust database filled with automated FAQs, initiates a cascade of help, providing articulate guidance almost akin to having a tech-savvy companion by your side, offering support every step of the way.

The allure of these AI systems stems from their capacity to furnish real-time support elegantly. Envision a scenario where a chatbot masterfully juggles inquiries regarding order statuses or nuances of return policies. With prompts shepherding these interactions, immediate answers emerge almost effortlessly, drastically cutting down on wait times and amplifying customer satisfaction. Creating these prompts demands more than technical know-how—it requires a balance of clarity, conciseness, and foresight into the customer's needs. This endeavor extends beyond simple question-answer exchanges, aiming to forge a seamless, engaging experience that mirrors the attentiveness of a personal consultation.

Now, diving deeper into the strategic side, optimizing customer service prompts blends precision with empathy. Start with a deep dive into understanding common customer pain points—insights that are invaluable when crafting prompts designed to quench these issues before they ignite into larger problems. Picture a common issue: frequent queries on shipping delays. Here, proactive prompts, like "Eager to know the status of your order? Click to check here," can preemptively ease frustration. Techniques for personalization further embellish the experience; analyzing past interactions enables AI to sculpt responses tailored to individual preferences, making each engagement feel custom-crafted and boutique-like.

The beneficial ripple effects of prompt engineering in the realm of customer service are expansive. A noticeable reduction in wait times, coupled with heightened resolution rates, culminates in happier customers. Yet, it's a boon that travels further. Improved dialogues with customers kindle loyalty and retention; an audience that feels both heard and cherished is inherently more inclined to return and endorse your services to others. This cascading wave transforms infrequent buyers into long-term proponents for your brand.

Moreover, integration with CRM systems elevates this advantage to dizzying heights. Infusing AI prompts with customer relationship management tools unlocks insights into consumer behavior that were previously elusive. Envision an agent entering a session with access to a dashboard revealing real-time data on customer interactions, allowing them to adjust their approach with surgical precision. A practical application of this involves integrating AI prompts alongside CRM for adept data collection—not only for tracking customer inclinations but also for forecasting future needs. Consequently, businesses can proffer more personalized solutions, propelling sales and expanding customer fidelity (source: Talkdesk).

Exercise: Analyze Your Customer Interaction

Reflect upon a recent interaction you've had with customer service, whether it evoked satisfaction or disappointment. What elements were particularly memorable or impactful? Analyze how prompt engineering could have refined or transformed that interaction. Identify and jot down three distinct aspects where thoughtfully constructed prompts could have notably altered your experience for the better.

Prompt engineering in the sphere of customer service is progressively reshaping the landscape of business-client interactions. It transcends mere technological solutions; it is an enabler, crafting deeply meaningful connections that resonate on a personal scale with customers. As you navigate through these applications, imagine how you might harness prompt engineering to enhance your own interactions, forging connections that are not merely efficient, but profoundly memorable and impactful.

Leveraging Prompts for Content Creation and Marketing

Imagine sitting at your desk, the aroma of freshly brewed coffee wafting through the air, as you ponder the intimidating blank document on your digital canvas. The task at hand is to generate fresh, captivating blog post ideas that engage your audience and leave a lasting impact. This is precisely where prompt engineering emerges as a trusty guide, steering you through the vast seas of creativity with unerring precision. By simply inputting a prompt such as "Generate blog post ideas about sustainable living," the AI at your fingertips can conjure a wonderful array of engaging topics. These ideas range from detailed explorations like "DIY Projects for a Greener Home" to insightful dissections such as "The Impact of Fast Fashion on the Environment." It's like having a brainstorming partner who is perpetually inspired and remarkably resilient, never running out of fresh angles to explore.

However, the utility of prompts extends far beyond merely generating ideas—they are instrumental in the actual crafting of content as well. Take social media, a realm where brevity must marry impactful messaging to succeed. Employing a prompt such as "Create a tweet about our new product launch" can lead to the birth of concise yet catchy posts that effortlessly capture a reader's fleeting attention. The AI does not work in isolation; it thoroughly evaluates your distinct brand voice along with the target audience, generating content that resonates deeply without forfeiting brand identity. Through this synergy between the boundless realm of human creativity and the steadfast efficiency of AI, the result is content that's both authentically engaging and strategically sound, ensuring each post hits the mark effectively.

Switching gears to the expansive realm of marketing campaigns, personalization becomes a pivotal, transformative factor. Instead of relying on generic communication, envision utilizing prompts to tailor each interaction uniquely. For example, "Write an email inviting Emily to our winter sale with a personal touch" prompts the AI to craft messages that resonate with a personal warmth, creating a sense of exclusivity. By addressing individual preferences and acknowledging past interactions, these emails transcend mere promotion, evolving into genuine conversations that lay the foundation for relationships built on trust and loyalty.

Search engine optimization (SEO) represents yet another area where AI's capabilities shine brilliantly. With the right prompts, AI-driven tools can deftly suggest keywords that amplify visibility without the pitfalls of content overstuffing. Picture querying, "What are trending keywords for eco-friendly products?" The AI, in response, meticulously analyzes current search trends and presents impactful phrases like "sustainable packaging" or "green energy solutions." Seamlessly weaving these keywords into your content elevates its reach exponentially, making it more accessible to potential customers actively seeking what your brand offers.

For those with a flair for storytelling, prompts act as a portal to unlock narratives brimming with untapped potential. Whether drafting a novel or constructing a marketing campaign interwoven with an engaging storyline, AI becomes a crucial ally in framing compelling arcs. Visualize inputting "Create a plot for a mystery novel set in Victorian London," and receiving a full-fledged outline teeming with unexpected twists and rich character development. The AI provides a foundational structure that empowers you to infuse intricate details, ensuring narratives are not only engaging but also coherently unified from beginning to end.

In the realm of creative content development, prompts serve as powerful catalysts for boundless innovation. They push the boundaries of conventional thought while respecting necessary constraints, offering fresh perspectives on familiar themes and reframing them in novel ways (source: Qurtoo). Imagine a prompt like "Craft a short story about a future where humans communicate through technology." With its boundless creativity, the AI generates imaginative scenarios that both challenge and inspire you to explore uncharted territories, sparking innovative ideas that inject vibrant life into each project you undertake.

Understanding these extensive applications is paramount for anyone venturing into the dynamic arena of content creation and marketing. With persistent practice, manipulating prompts becomes second nature, seamlessly integrating into your creative workflow. They possess the transformative power to turn daunting tasks into approachable endeavors, offering clarity amidst potential chaos. As you delve into these vast possibilities, remember that prompts are not merely procedural tools—they are indispensable partners in the journey of innovation, guiding, inspiring, and aiding you at every step of your creative process.

Monetizing Your Skills: Freelancing and Consulting

Imagine the liberating sensation of waking up each morning without the constraints of adhering to a conventional nine-to-five schedule, and instead, exercising full autonomy over your professional life. This is the enticing promise of freelancing, where the world becomes your oyster and you hold the reins to your career. In the ever-expanding universe of freelance work, one field stands out as particularly ripe with opportunity: prompt engineering. As artificial intelligence continues to expand its reach into all corners of business, driving efficiency and pioneering innovation, the demand for skilled prompt engineers has surged significantly. This growing field offers a wealth of possibilities for those with the prowess to enhance AI systems.

Online platforms such as Upwork and Freelancer have transformed into bustling digital marketplaces. Within these virtual spaces, professionals who possess strong expertise in prompt engineering can seamlessly connect with clients eagerly searching for their talents. Tech companies, perpetually evolving and innovating, are on the constant hunt for specialists who can fine-tune their AI's conversational prowess, enabling more natural interactions. Marketing firms, in their quest to craft resonant and effective narratives, seek adept craftsmen to generate content that truly connects with target audiences. Even sectors like customer service, which look to optimize their automated interactions, frequently turn to prompt engineers to fine-tune their systems, ensuring customer experiences are fluid, efficient, and reflect a more human touch.

Transitioning from merely understanding your craft to forging a viable livelihood from it requires strategic planning and a touch of entrepreneurial spirit. Initiating a consulting business provides a somewhat more robust and formalized structure than freelancing, yet it can be equally rewarding in terms of both personal satisfaction and financial gain. The journey begins by defining your niche within the vast landscape of AI and prompt engineering. Are you adept at creating chatbots that mimic human conversation with extraordinary precision? Or is your forte embedded in AI-driven marketing solutions that can transform business outreach strategies? Clearly pinpointing your specialty not only aids in targeting the appropriate clients but also aligns your services more effectively with market demands.

Establishing your brand is the next pivotal step in this process. This involves selecting a compelling business name that echoes your mission and values, designing an appealing logo, and, crucially, constructing a professional and polished website. Your digital presence should be a mirror of your capabilities, effectively communicating your services and showcasing your expertise. Utilize blogs to demonstrate thought leadership, share detailed case studies to provide tangible proof of your competencies, or assemble a portfolio that highlights past successes and sets you apart from the competition.

There's an art to pricing your services, which involves balancing the fees you charge with the value you can deliver. Pricing models should be adaptable to the variety of client needs you may encounter. Hourly rates are suitable for projects where scope might change over time, enabling you to adjust as needed. For projects with a fixed scope, project-based fees allow clients to understand total costs upfront, making these arrangements more palatable for those averse to unpredictability. As your career progresses and your reputation solidifies, embrace the opportunity to recalibrate your rates, ensuring they accurately reflect your burgeoning expertise and the substantial value you provide.

Running a successful consulting business transcends having technical skills alone; it also requires building a robust network of professional connections. Engaging actively in industry conferences, joining AI-centric forums, and participating in relevant webinars are invaluable for connecting with a community of like-minded professionals and potential clients. Your online presence can often serve as a more compelling calling card than any printed business card. Platforms such as LinkedIn can be instrumental in this aspect, allowing you to present your skills, share incisive insights through articles, and actively engage with peers in your domain. This not only bolsters your position as a recognized expert but also fosters opportunities for collaborations and client referrals, further expanding your professional opportunities.

As you delve into this exhilarating journey, bear in mind that cultivating and bolstering your personal brand demands dedication and energy but is an investment well worth making. An illustrious brand does more than just attract clientele; it engenders trust and imbues you with credibility—both vital components for achieving sustained success in the competitive realm of consulting. The road may be long, yet each step fortifies the foundation of a brand that will, in time, reap abundant rewards.

Industry Applications: Healthcare, Education, and Beyond

In healthcare, prompts are revolutionizing patient interaction and data analysis, offering a new dimension to medical care. Imagine a virtual health assistant that not only schedules your appointments but also reminds you to take medication, tracks symptoms, and even provides dietary suggestions based on your health records. These assistants operate through carefully crafted prompts, responding to patient queries with precision and empathy. By analyzing patient data, they predict potential health issues before they escalate, offering preventive measures that can save lives. Virtual health assistants are rapidly becoming an integral part of patient care, enhancing both efficiency and personalization in medical services.

In the educational landscape, AI prompts are transforming how students learn and interact with educational content. Adaptive learning systems use these prompts to tailor educational experiences to each student's needs, creating a personalized learning environment. Picture a student struggling with algebra—AI tools analyze their learning patterns and adapt lessons in real-time, ensuring that concepts are grasped at the student's pace. This personalized approach not only improves comprehension but also boosts confidence, making learning more accessible and engaging. Educational platforms are now equipped with interactive exercises and quizzes, designed to adapt based on the student's progress and performance, ensuring that learning remains dynamic and effective.

Beyond healthcare and education, prompt engineering is making waves in industries such as finance, retail, and logistics. In finance, AI-driven prompts assist advisors by analyzing market trends and client portfolios, offering insights and recommendations that enhance decision-making processes. For instance, a financial advisor might receive alerts about potential investment opportunities tailored to specific client goals. In retail, AI enhances the customer experience by providing personalized shopping recommendations based on browsing history and preferences. By integrating prompts into retail systems, businesses can offer real-time assistance to shoppers, guiding them through their purchasing journey with ease.

Prompt engineering also plays a pivotal role in logistics, optimizing supply chain operations through precise data analysis and predictive modeling. By using AI-driven prompts to forecast demand and manage inventory levels, companies can streamline operations and reduce waste. This not only improves efficiency but also boosts profitability by ensuring that resources are allocated effectively. Logistics firms benefit from enhanced tracking capabilities and improved coordination between various stakeholders, resulting in smoother operations and increased customer satisfaction.

Cross-industry innovations showcase how prompt engineering can transcend traditional boundaries, fostering collaboration between sectors. For example, techniques developed in healthcare for data analysis and patient interaction can be adapted to improve customer service in retail settings. Similarly, AI models used for financial forecasting can enhance supply chain management in logistics. These cross-industry applications illustrate the versatility of prompt engineering, demonstrating how innovations in one field can drive advancements in others.

Case studies highlight successful cross-industry applications of prompt engineering. In one instance, a healthcare provider leveraged AI prompts originally designed for financial risk assessment to predict patient outcomes. By adapting these prompts for medical use, they improved diagnostic accuracy and patient care significantly. In another case, a retail chain used AI-driven insights from logistics to optimize inventory management, reducing costs while maintaining product availability. These examples underscore the potential of prompt engineering to create value across diverse sectors.

The adaptability of prompt engineering to various industries underscores its transformative potential. Whether enhancing patient care, personalizing education, or optimizing business operations, prompts provide the foundation for smarter interactions and more informed decisions. As technology continues to evolve, the possibilities for prompt engineering are boundless, offering innovative solutions that address complex challenges in creative ways. The future holds exciting prospects for those ready to explore the myriad applications of prompt engineering across different domains.

Building AI-Driven Business Models

Creating a business centered around artificial intelligence is akin to launching a venture with formidable capabilities right from the outset. Envision the task of pinpointing those elusive market gaps where AI technology can effortlessly intervene and manifest its transformative powers. Consider industries replete with monotonous, repetitive tasks or sectors where data analysis poses as a cumbersome challenge. In these domains, AI demonstrates its potential with unmatched brilliance, with the nuance of prompt engineering playing a crucial role. Picture a business model designed around AI tools that conduct mundane tasks, liberating the human intellect to delve into more creative and impactful pursuits. Imagine deploying AI within an industry such as real estate, a field where technology can not only automate listings but also offer personalized property suggestions carefully tailored to meet individualized client preferences. These ingeniously crafted solutions address the overlooked deficiencies of traditional methodologies, rendering your business not only innovative but utterly essential.

Prompts take on a critical role in refining business strategy, functioning as the silent yet powerful influence that steers intelligent decision-making in new directions. They form the backbone of AI-led market analysis, offering insights that are indispensable for informed strategic planning. Picture a sophisticated dashboard where prompts instruct the AI to comb through vast reservoirs of market data, distilling trends and patterns to illuminate the path forward for your business. This analysis extends beyond mere number crunching; it paints a comprehensive portrait of potential opportunities and dictates which strategic directions to follow. By aligning these insights with your organizational objectives, you forge a strategy that is not only rich with data but also robustly agile and keenly forward-thinking.

The spectrum of revenue streams generated from AI offerings is as vast as it is financially rewarding. Subscription services for AI tools emerge as a particularly reliable revenue model. Clients commit to a monthly fee in exchange for access to cutting-edge AI solutions designed to streamline operations, delivering value that is both obvious and persuasive. Reflect upon software as a service (SaaS) platforms that deploy AI to heighten productivity or operational efficiency—consider automated accounting tools or marketing analytics platforms that supply real-time insights. These services not only maintain a reliable income flow but also guarantee that clients receive ongoing enhancements and support. This symbiotic model proves advantageous for both the business, sustaining a recurring revenue, and the customer, who benefits from perpetual assistance and innovation.

Success within AI business models frequently relies heavily on innovation and adaptability. Let us delve deeper into exemplary startups that have seamlessly woven AI into their fundamental offerings. Consider, for instance, a pioneering tech startup that harnessed AI to transform our understanding of health data. Through utilizing prompts to expedite and refine patient data collection and analysis, they furnished healthcare providers with actionable insights that could be translated into improved patient care. This innovation not only elevated health outcomes but also established the startup as a trailblazer in health tech advancement.

Turning to another inspiring instance, we find a logistics company that successfully employed AI to optimize delivery routes, curtailing fuel expenses and significantly reducing delivery times. By leveraging prompts, they fine-tuned algorithms capable of predicting traffic patterns and optimizing routes in real-time, amplifying efficiency while enhancing customer satisfaction through punctual deliveries. These success narratives underscore the paramount importance of fully integrating AI into your core business operations rather than relegating it to a secondary role.

Understanding these illustrative examples provides a comprehensive blueprint for crafting your AI-driven business model. It's about looking beyond immediate profits and focusing on sustained growth and enduring adaptability. These businesses didn't merely adopt AI—they enshrined it into their very essence, enabling them to swiftly adjust to market shifts. Such adaptability frequently distinguishes thriving enterprises within rapidly evolving landscapes.

Throughout this exploration of AI-driven business models, one persistent theme emerges: the undeniable power of prompts in propelling innovation and efficiency. Whether identifying market gaps, devising strategic frameworks, or conceptualizing new revenue streams, prompts are invaluable allies in extracting AI's vast potential. They guide decision-making, streamline operations, and unveil fresh growth opportunities.

Integrating these elements into your enterprise not only sets a course towards success but also positions you prominently within an intensely competitive field. As you navigate the realm of AI-centric businesses, remember that prompts are not simply tools; they're catalysts for profound change, driving your business forward with unwavering purpose and precision.

Case Studies: Monetization Success Stories

In the ever-evolving realm of AI, real-world success stories serve as beacons, illuminating the path toward financial prosperity through prompt engineering. Consider the case of an AI consulting firm that skyrocketed from a modest startup to an industry leader. This firm stands as a testament to the transformative power of prompt engineering when strategically applied.

Initially, they focused on small-scale projects, harnessing AI to streamline business processes for local enterprises. Their commitment to excellence and client-centric approach soon earned them a sterling reputation. Word of mouth and strategic networking played pivotal roles in their exponential growth, allowing them to expand their clientele across various sectors, including finance and healthcare.

Key strategies implemented by this firm involved a robust focus on client engagement. They understood that building trust and maintaining open communication channels were paramount. Regular check-ins and feedback sessions ensured that their solutions remained aligned with client objectives, fostering long-lasting partnerships. Additionally, they offered tailored AI solutions, adapting their services to meet the unique needs of each client. This flexibility not only increased customer satisfaction but also opened doors to new opportunities, as satisfied clients became enthusiastic advocates.

From these success stories, several valuable lessons emerge. Continuous learning and adaptation proved crucial. The firm consistently invested in up-skilling their team, ensuring they stayed ahead of AI trends and technological advancements. This proactive approach allowed them to offer cutting-edge solutions that resonated with modern business challenges. Moreover, they embraced innovation, experimenting with novel AI applications beyond conventional boundaries. Their willingness to explore uncharted territories set them apart from competitors and attracted clients eager for creative solutions.

For those embarking on their own monetization journey, these insights underscore the importance of agility and foresight. Embracing a growth mindset and remaining receptive to change can significantly enhance your prospects in the dynamic world of AI. Furthermore, fostering strong client relationships through personalized service and transparent communication can build a loyal customer base that fuels sustainable success.

Looking to the future, the landscape of prompt engineering continues to evolve, offering exciting monetization opportunities. Emerging markets and technologies present fertile ground for exploration. Industries such as agriculture are increasingly turning to AI for precision farming solutions, creating demand for prompt engineers who can tailor AI models to specific agricultural needs. Additionally, as environmental concerns grow, the renewable energy sector seeks innovative ways to optimize energy consumption and reduce waste through AI-driven insights.

The rise of edge computing—a paradigm shifting data processing closer to its source—promises new avenues for prompt engineering monetization. By developing AI models that operate seamlessly on edge devices, prompt engineers can tap into sectors like IoT and smart cities, where real-time data analysis is crucial. As businesses strive for efficiency and sustainability, the demand for AI solutions that integrate seamlessly into existing infrastructures will only increase.

In conclusion, the synergy between prompt engineering and monetization is a powerful force shaping the future of AI-driven businesses. By drawing inspiration from successful case studies and embracing innovation, aspiring professionals can carve their own path toward financial success. The lessons learned from established firms underscore the significance of adaptability, continuous learning, and client engagement in achieving lasting impact.

As we transition into the next chapter, we will explore how prompt engineering can be leveraged to drive innovation and efficiency across various industries. By understanding the broader implications of AI applications, you'll gain valuable insights into how these technologies can transform traditional business models and pave the way for a more connected future. Buckle up as we delve deeper into the transformative potential of AI in reshaping industries worldwide.

Maintaining Consistency in AI Responses

Imagine, if you will, the anticipation that builds as you approach your favorite coffee shop, knowing exactly what aromatic delight awaits you—a cup crafted with precision, bringing a sense of warmth and familiarity. Now, picture the unexpected surprise, akin to walking through that door and receiving, not the anticipated frothy cappuccino, but an unrecognizable mixture that varies entirely from your expected indulgence. Such a situation mirrors the user experience when artificial intelligence fails to deliver consistent responses. In the realm of AI, maintaining a uniformity of output goes beyond being a mere feature; it encapsulates the quintessential element of ensuring trustworthiness and steadfast reliability.

This consistent delivery becomes particularly crucial within the realm of customer service and support chatbots. Here, even an isolated response that deviates from the norm could potentially sow seeds of confusion among users and inadvertently tarnish the esteemed credibility of a brand. In our rapidly evolving digital landscape, where interactions are quicker and stakes are perpetually higher, consistency emerges as the bedrock principle underpinning brand identity and the tenant of enduring customer loyalty. It is imperative that your chatbot not only adheres to a dependable tone but continues it seamlessly, whether it tackles a straightforward query or navigates the complexities of multifaceted issues.

To construct a robust foundation for consistency, the standardization of prompt language emerges as the keystone. Standardized prompts operate akin to a universal code—a lexicon mutually comprehended by both AI systems and end-users. By ensuring that interactions are built upon a common expanse of language continuity, AI is directed towards the generation of responses that anchor firmly in reliability, effectively minimizing potential for misinterpretation and misunderstanding. Establishing concrete guidelines, delineating tone and stylistic choices, further facilitates a harmonious alignment of AI's and brand's voices across disparate platforms. Whether your brand exudes an aura of playful exuberance or staunch professionalism, saturation of these guidelines ensures that the AI echoes the brand's intended personality with precision, fostering a seamless, unified user experience that transcends individual interactions.

Integrating feedback loops within your strategic framework is another pivotal component. These loops effectively act as an analytic instrument—a magnifying glass granting visibility into areas where AI might inadvertently diverge from the desired course. By implementing robust mechanisms that allow users to rate or comment on interactions, the feedback gathered transforms into a repository of invaluable data. This compendium of insights serves as a navigational aid for improvements and fine-tuning of AI responses. Consider this akin to a master chef tasting every iteration of a dish to ensure the symphony of flavors achieves just the right balance. Through steady streams of consistent user feedback, prompts can be meticulously refined, responses adeptly tuned, facilitating an alignment that closely mirrors user expectations.

However, despite these concerted efforts and careful strategies, the pursuit of consistency is not devoid of its inherent challenges. AI models and the data fueling them exist in dynamic environs, constantly evolving and updating in concordance with new technological capabilities, thereby impacting emergent response patterns. Enduring in such a fluid landscape demands a principle of vigilance and an adaptable posture. Regularly reviewing and adjusting prompts to cater to novel model capabilities and emerging data insights proves crucial. This proactive, vigilant approach ensures that your AI retains its efficacious response capabilities even as landscapes shift and evolve inexorably.

In light of these considerations, consider a practical exercise—an Interactive Element: Consistency Check Quiz. Engage with your existing AI framework by crafting a checklist punctuating elements underpinning consistent responses. Enumerate factors such as tonal cohesion, linguistic uniformity, and the presence or absence of effective feedback mechanisms. Subsequently, assign a rating to each element based on a scale from 1 to 5, wherein 1 signifies the presence of inconsistency and 5 denotes robust consistency. Such a diagnostic exercise will illuminate areas necessitating attention and guide your efforts toward refining and optimizing your AI strategy.

To encapsulate, maintaining consistency in AI responses hinges on establishing formidable standards, weaving in feedback mechanisms, and exercising adaptability to cope with inevitable changes. It's an endeavor focused on crafting an environment where users genuinely feel understood and deeply valued, akin to that enduring satisfaction of savoring the perfectly crafted cappuccino they anticipate each visit to their cherished café. It's more than just technology; it's about crafting experiences that resonate, and comfort like familiar aromas of a dependable brew.

Efficiency Tips for Prompt Engineers

Prompt engineering, much like any craft, benefits from efficiency. Let's explore some strategies to streamline your process and boost productivity. One effective technique is batch processing. Think of it as preparing meals for the week on a Sunday afternoon. You set aside time to tackle a group of prompts in one go, which minimizes the need to switch between different tasks. This focused effort reduces mental fatigue and allows for a more consistent thought process. You create a rhythm, a cadence, that keeps your mind engaged and reduces the scatter of constant context-switching.

Utilizing templates is another game-changer. Imagine having a blueprint for common queries ready at your fingertips. Templates act as a solid foundation, giving you a head start and allowing you to customize as needed without starting from scratch every time. This approach not only saves precious minutes but also ensures consistency in the basic structure of your prompts. Templates can be both specific and adaptable, accommodating various scenarios with just minor tweaks. They serve as your trusty sidekick, always ready to lend a hand when creativity decides to take a break.

When it comes to prioritizing tasks, focusing on high-value prompts is key. Not all prompts are created equal; some have a greater impact on your objectives than others. It's crucial to identify which prompts advance your goals most effectively and prioritize those. Consider the 80/20 rule—80% of your outcomes come from 20% of your efforts. Apply this principle to prompt engineering by identifying the prompts that yield the most significant results and dedicating your energy there. This strategic focus ensures that your efforts are not just busy work but purposeful and impactful.

Automation tools are invaluable allies in managing repetitive tasks. Automation scripts can be set up for prompt testing, allowing you to run multiple tests without manually handling each one. These scripts free up your mental bandwidth, enabling you to focus on more complex and creative aspects of prompt engineering. Imagine having a virtual assistant that takes care of the mundane so you can concentrate on innovation. Automation also reduces the chance of human error, providing more reliable and consistent outcomes.

Reducing cognitive load is vital for sustaining long-term productivity. Your brain, like any muscle, needs rest to function optimally. Breaks are not just beneficial; they're necessary. Implement strategies like the Pomodoro technique—work intensely for 25 minutes, then rest for 5. This cycle keeps your mind fresh and prevents burnout. Time management also plays a crucial role. Allocate specific times for focused work and others for lighter tasks or relaxation. Balancing work with periods of rest ensures sustained creativity and mental acuity.

Interactive Element: Efficiency Checklist

Create an efficiency checklist tailored to your workflow. Include steps like setting up templates, scheduling regular breaks, and prioritizing high-impact prompts. Use this checklist to evaluate your daily routine and identify areas for improvement.

Remember, efficiency in prompt engineering isn't about rushing through tasks but optimizing how you approach them. By integrating batch processing, templates, task prioritization, automation tools, and cognitive load management, you lay the groundwork for a productive and sustainable practice. As you navigate this field, these strategies will not only enhance your output but also enrich your experience, ensuring you maintain both quality and enthusiasm in your work.

Optimizing Prompts for Different AI Platforms

Navigating the diverse landscape of AI platforms is akin to exploring a vibrant tapestry woven with distinct threads. Each platform represents a unique strand, offering subtle yet impactful variations that require a discerning approach to fully understand and utilize. Consider ChatGPT and Claude as two siblings with distinctive yet complementary talents, each contributing valuable skills to the family portfolio. ChatGPT thrives on conversational nuances, an adept communicator that excels in scenarios demanding intricate dialogue and interactive exchange. It's the perfect choice for complex discussions or scenarios where the nuance of human-like conversation enhances understanding, such as customer service interactions or creative brainstorming sessions.

Meanwhile, Claude stands out in its forte of structured data processing, seamlessly excelling in tasks that revolve around comprehensive data analysis and meticulous report generation. Think of Claude as a methodical analyst who, with a keen eye for detail, synthesizes information into digestible insights. Tailoring your prompts to capitalize on these distinct capabilities ensures you harness their maximum potential effectively and efficiently. For instance, presenting ChatGPT with a prompt to "Discuss the benefits of remote work" will initiate a rich, textured conversation delving deep into the various facets and implications. Conversely, entrusting Claude with "Analyze remote work trends from 2020 to 2023" will result in a structured, data-driven exploration of patterns and shifts in the workforce landscape during those years.

Voice-activated AI systems introduce an additional layer of complexity to this landscape, requiring thoughtful prompts that account for vocal intonations, pace shifts, and the nuances of real-time auditory processing. Imagine engaging with a voice assistant for weather updates. While a succinct prompt like "What's the weather?" suffices, enriching the query with specific context—such as "What's the weather like this weekend in New York?"—provides a more nuanced and precise response. This level of specificity not only augments the accuracy of the information provided but also enhances the overall user satisfaction. Recognizing these subtle differences and judiciously adapting prompts in response is key to optimizing performance across voice-enabled platforms.

Achieving cross-platform consistency is an art form unto itself. It's about orchestrating a seamless and unified experience that is harmonious for users, regardless of the system with which they interact. The cornerstone of achieving this consistency lies in the harmonization of prompt language and structure. Envision maintaining a cohesive tone across platforms—whether it skews towards formal, leans into casual, or strikes a balance between the two. This uniformity of tone and style ensures users experience an element of familiarity with every interaction, no matter the device or platform. It parallels speaking multiple languages but with the same signature accent, an approach that nurtures trust and comfort.

Delving deeper into the intricacies of these platforms reveals unique features that can be leveraged to enhance prompt engineering, breathing life into innovative functionalities. Specialized APIs, for instance, serve as powerful conduits to advanced capabilities and functionalities. These interfaces act as gateways that enable you to tap into tailored abilities within a platform, such as integrating external data sources or utilizing powerful processing techniques. For example, employing an API to incorporate real-time data into your prompts can transform responses into dynamic, live-informed communications. This sophisticated integration broadens the horizons for creating more robust, responsive, and context-aware AI applications.

This potential for integration extends beyond the obvious. By ingeniously linking AI prompts with other systems and tools, you can expand capabilities and streamline complex operations. Envision a scenario where AI integrates with CRM systems to enable seamless automated customer interactions that are not only meticulously efficient but also uniquely personalized. Picture an AI that accesses customer data to refine and personalize its responses during support interactions, creating an experience that is customized and feels genuinely attentive. This synergy between AI and existing systems revolutionizes business operations, enhancing both operational efficiency and the quality of user interactions.

As you refine your approach to prompt engineering across diverse platforms, consider these strategies to be the essential tools in your expanding toolkit. Tailoring prompts to suit specific platform strengths not only optimizes efficiency and performance but also enhances the richness and depth of user interactions. Whether you are leveraging APIs for enhanced, seamless functionality or integrating prompts with CRM systems for smoother operations, these techniques ensure that your AI applications are not only effective but also groundbreaking in their innovation. The diverse tapestry of AI platforms presents a wealth of opportunities ripe for exploration and exploitation, paving the way for richer interactions and more meaningful outcomes.

Balancing Creativity and Structure in Prompts

Imagine you're a painter standing in front of a blank canvas. The freedom to create anything is exhilarating, yet daunting. This is what prompt crafting can feel like—balancing between free-spirited creativity and methodical structure. Striking the right balance is akin to a dance where flexibility and rigor sway together, creating prompts that resonate with users and fulfill technical needs.

Flexibility allows creative content to breathe. It's about letting your imagination stretch the boundaries of what's possible. Think of generating story ideas or engaging social media posts. Here, creativity fuels innovation, sparking fresh concepts and perspectives that captivate audiences. However, without structure, creativity can wander aimlessly, leading to outputs that lack focus. Structure ensures that creative ideas are grounded, channeling them into coherent responses that meet specific goals.

When it comes to technical or factual prompts, structure takes the lead. You need precision and clarity to ensure the AI provides accurate information. But even here, a touch of creativity can enhance engagement—turning standard data requests into interactive experiences that invite curiosity. For instance, turning a straightforward data request into a scenario-based query adds an element of intrigue while maintaining accuracy.

To encourage creativity without losing structure, consider hosting brainstorming sessions where ideas flow freely without judgment. Use mind mapping tools to visualize connections between concepts, allowing fresh insights to emerge organically. This process not only inspires creativity but also reveals patterns that can guide structured prompt development. Think of it as sketching out ideas before committing to a final piece—a safe space where trial and error lead to innovation.

Structured frameworks act as scaffolding for creative endeavors. They provide a foundation upon which creativity can flourish without becoming chaotic. In storytelling prompts, for example, frameworks offer a roadmap—

defining characters, settings, and plot elements that give stories shape while leaving room for imaginative twists. By setting parameters within which creativity can roam, frameworks ensure that prompts remain coherent and aligned with objectives.

Successful examples of balancing creativity and structure abound in marketing campaigns that capture attention while delivering clear messages. Consider a campaign for a new product launch: the creative aspect might involve crafting engaging narratives that resonate emotionally with consumers. Meanwhile, structured elements ensure these narratives align with brand messaging and convey key product features effectively.

In one successful campaign, a company used creative storytelling to introduce their eco-friendly product line. They crafted a narrative around a character's journey toward sustainable living—engaging audiences emotionally while subtly highlighting product benefits. The structured framework ensured consistency across platforms and messages, resulting in increased brand awareness and consumer engagement.

Reflect on how creativity and structure interplay in different domains. Whether you're crafting prompts for educational tools or developing marketing strategies, this balance is crucial for effective communication with AI systems. By fostering environments where creativity thrives within structured boundaries, you unlock the full potential of prompt engineering.

Think about how you can apply these principles in your work. Encourage collaboration among team members to generate diverse ideas while maintaining alignment with project goals. Embrace flexibility when exploring new concepts but rely on structured frameworks to keep efforts focused and productive.

Balancing creativity and structure isn't just about finding middle ground; it's about recognizing their complementary roles in enhancing prompts' impactfulness. Creativity breathes life into prompts, making them engaging and relatable. Structure provides direction—ensuring outputs are meaningful and aligned with intended purposes.

As you experiment with different approaches to prompt crafting, remember that both elements have vital roles in shaping successful interactions between humans and AI systems. Embrace the dance between flexibility and rigor—where every step taken leads closer to achieving your desired outcomes in prompt engineering endeavors.

Tools and Software to Enhance Prompt Engineering

Imagine you're a writer sitting at your desk, surrounded by an array of tools—each designed to refine your craft and make your process more efficient. In the realm of prompt engineering, it's much the same. The right software tools can transform your approach from good to exceptional. AI-specific text editors are like the proverbial "Swiss Army knife" for prompt engineers. These editors often come equipped with features tailored for AI interactions—such as syntax highlighting and auto-completion—that streamline the prompt creation process. They also provide real-time feedback on grammar and style, ensuring clarity and coherence in your prompts.

Collaborative platforms take this one step further by allowing teams to work together seamlessly on prompt projects. Picture a digital workspace where you and your colleagues can brainstorm, draft, and refine prompts collectively. These platforms facilitate communication and coordination, making it easier to align on tone, style, and objectives. Imagine a scenario where you're crafting prompts for a marketing campaign; having input from multiple team members ensures a well-rounded approach that resonates with diverse audiences.

Using advanced tools offers numerous benefits in prompt engineering. Grammar and style checks are invaluable for maintaining high-quality outputs. They catch errors you might overlook during manual reviews, ensuring that your prompts are polished and professional. Moreover, these tools often come with analytics features that help assess prompt performance, providing insights into which prompts are most effective. This data-driven approach allows you to refine your strategies based on concrete evidence rather than guesswork.

Selecting the right software is crucial for maximizing these benefits. Consider your specific needs and goals when evaluating options. Compatibility with various AI platforms is a key factor; you want tools that work seamlessly with the systems you're using. Additionally, look for software with user-friendly interfaces that don't require extensive training to navigate. The goal is to enhance your workflow, not complicate it.

As technology evolves, emerging tools promise to revolutionize prompt engineering further. AI-driven analytics tools are on the rise, offering deeper insights into prompt performance than ever before. These tools analyze vast datasets to identify patterns and trends, helping you fine-tune your prompts for optimal engagement and effectiveness. Picture having access to a dashboard that visualizes how different prompts perform across various platforms and audiences—empowering you to make informed decisions about future strategies.

In this rapidly changing landscape, staying updated with new developments is essential. Subscribe to industry newsletters or join online communities where professionals discuss the latest tools and technologies. Engaging with these resources keeps you informed about emerging trends and best practices in prompt engineering.

The beauty of technology lies in its ability to simplify complex processes—and prompt engineering is no exception. With the right tools at your disposal, you can streamline your workflow, enhance the quality of your outputs, and ultimately achieve more impactful results. Whether you're working solo or as part of a team, leveraging software designed specifically for prompt engineering can elevate your practice to new heights.

Visual Element: Software Tools Comparison Chart

Consider creating a comparison chart of popular prompt engineering tools. Include features like grammar checks, AI compatibility, user interface, and analytics capabilities. This visual aid will help you quickly assess which tools align best with your needs and preferences.

As you explore different software options, remember that the goal is not merely to adopt every new tool available but to find those that genuinely enhance your process. The right combination of tools can transform prompt engineering from a challenging task into an engaging and rewarding endeavor—one where creativity flourishes alongside efficiency.

Creating a Personal Prompt Library

Creating a personal prompt library can truly be a transformative step in revolutionizing your ability to work more efficiently and consistently in the innovative world of prompt engineering. Imagine the sheer ease and satisfaction that comes from having immediate access to your most frequently utilized and meticulously crafted prompts, much like effortlessly reaching for your preferred tool from an expertly organized toolbox. This personal library morphs into a centralized hub, a vital repository storing an array of prompts that you have diligently crafted and perfected over time. It transcends mere convenience, serving instead to streamline your workflow meticulously, while ensuring you possess an invaluable reservoir to draw upon whenever the need arises.

Organizing this personal library meticulously becomes paramount for maximizing its myriad benefits. It's worthwhile to consider categorizing your prompts based on specific industries or functions—a process akin to arranging your books into well-defined genres on an expansive shelf. In this way, whenever you're engrossed in a project forward in the healthcare sector, you can effortlessly locate the relevant prompts without wading through a sea of unrelated ones. Furthermore, the implementation of a robust tagging system substantially enhances accessibility. These tags function as indispensable signposts, deftly directing you to the appropriate prompt with the mere input of a keyword in a search. Such an organized system not only saves time but also minimizes frustration, enabling you to devote more attention to creative endeavors rather than administrative burdens.

Regular maintenance of your library ensures it remains a highly valuable tool rather than devolving into a stagnant archive. Consider setting a routine schedule for reviewing and updating your prompts consistently. This practice diligently ensures that your library remains vibrant and relevant, thus reflecting the latest trends and best practices in prompt engineering.

It's analogous to tending to a flourishing garden, where consistent care and attention foster growth and productivity. By routinely revisiting your prompts, you have the opportunity to refine them based on newfound insights, which ensures they continue to deliver on optimal results consistently.

Let us now delve into how this personal library can be efficiently leveraged across various scenarios. When involved in rapid prototyping and testing, possessing an extensive library expedites the process significantly. Instead of starting anew each time, you can effortlessly pull from existing prompts, making necessary adjustments with agility. This flexibility becomes invaluable in fast-paced environments where time is of the utmost essence. Moreover, when onboarding new team members, your well-curated library serves as an exemplary reference tool. It furnishes them with tried-and-true examples, fostering an understanding of the delicate nuances involved in crafting effective prompts. They can learn from past successes and circumvent potential pitfalls, thereby accelerating their learning curve.

Incorporating these efficient practices into your routine has the potential to completely transform your approach to prompt engineering. A well-maintained personal prompt library is certainly more than just a mere collection of words; it evolves into a strategic asset that empowers you to work not only smarter but also more effectively. As you continue to hone your skills and expand your library, you will find it becoming an indispensable aspect of your toolkit—a resource that evolves alongside you and tenaciously supports your growth as an adept prompt engineer.

As we draw this chapter to a close, reflecting on strategies designed for consistent efficiency, it is crucial to understand that these techniques transcend the mere optimization of individual tasks. They are centered around crafting a cohesive system that enhances your overall effectiveness significantly. By instituting consistency in AI responses, leveraging time-saving techniques to bolster efficiency, optimizing prompts for diverse platforms, maintaining the delicate balance between creativity and structure, and harnessing advanced tools, you are establishing a robust foundation for unrivaled success in prompt engineering. In the impending chapter, we'll explore the practical application of these principles in a variety of real-world scenarios across diverse industries. We will illuminate the transformative power of prompt engineering, bringing these strategies to life in captivating real-world applications. So, prepare yourself for more exhilarating insights as we delve into practical scenarios where these principles spring into action.

4

Matthew K Prompt Engineering for Beginners: Master AI, Prompt Engineering, ChatGPT, Claude, and More to Work Smarter and Earn Faster Review Request Page

Make a Difference with Your Review

Unlock the Power of Generosity

"Real strength has to do with helping others." – Fred Rogers

Imagine this: You're exploring the amazing world of AI—learning how to talk to smart tools like ChatGPT and Claude. Now picture someone else just like you, standing at the starting line, unsure of where to begin.

That's where you come in.

I wrote this book to make prompt engineering easy to understand, exciting to learn, and useful in real life—whether you want to save time, earn more, or just feel more confident using AI.

But here's the thing—your review can help others find this guide and start their own journey too.

Most people decide what to read based on what others say. That's why I'm asking you to leave a quick review. It only takes a minute, but it can make a huge difference. Your review might help...

- One more small business grow and give back to their town.
- One more worker land a job they're proud of.
- One more student feel excited to learn.
- One more parent start a new way to earn.
- One more dream take its very first step.

☞ To leave a review, just scan the QR code or visit this link:

https://www.amazon.com/review/review-your-purchases/?asin= B0F83NJ51X

If you enjoy learning and helping others, then you're exactly the kind of reader I hoped this book would reach.

Thank you so much for your support!

– Matthew K

5

Chapter 4: Overcoming Challenges and Building Confidence

Overcoming Fear of Technical Concepts

Imagine, if you will, standing at the entrance of an immense and seemingly endless library, its towering shelves filled with bound volumes, each embossed with mysterious symbols and texts written in an unfamiliar language. For many beginners who are embarking on the journey of understanding Artificial Intelligence (AI) and its associated technical jargon, this image can be an apt metaphor for their initial experience. The prospect of grappling with complex aspects such as advanced mathematics, intricate algorithms, and diverse data structures can indeed be overwhelming and intimidating. Often, individuals come under the impression that these skills are inherent, a natural gift that only a select few possess. However, it is crucial to dismantle this myth. The reality is that technical skills are not an endowment from birth, but rather they are painstakingly developed through a robust blend of curiosity, unwavering persistence, and consistent practice.

One pervasive fear that many learners encounter is the perceived intricacy of mathematical theories underlying AI. Terms such as "neural networks," "gradient descent," or "backpropagation" can sound alien and rather daunting.

Nevertheless, akin to the act of learning to ride a bicycle, those initial moments of instability and doubt pave the way to gradually building confidence through perseverance and practice. Misconceptions about the natural requirement for an inborn ability often act as a deterrent to many. However, attaining technical proficiency is akin to a marathon rather than a sprint—a journey marked by a succession of small, incremental steps and continual growth. Understanding inherently grows as one delves into the material, welcomes the process of inquiry, and embraces the inevitable mistakes that occur along the way.

To demystify these intriguing yet intimidating concepts, consider using more relatable analogies. For instance, envision algorithms as you would recipes in the culinary world. In much the same way that a recipe offers guidance through a sequence of steps required to bake a cake, an algorithm provides a structured set of instructions aimed at solving a particular problem. There is no sorcery involved—just a logical progression of steps. Similarly, AI models can be likened to chefs honing their craft by practicing an array of recipes over time. As they practice, their culinary skills improve, allowing them to create delectable dishes and adapt to a variety of new ingredients seamlessly.

The cultivation of a growth mindset becomes a pivotal component in overcoming such fears. Embrace wholeheartedly the notion that expertise develops with the dedication of effort and increased commitment. In this context, progress takes precedence over an elusive notion of perfection, and every small success builds momentum leading to even greater accomplishments. Celebrate these successes and bear in mind that everyone commences their journey from a starting point. Mistakes, rather than being seen as setbacks, should be recognized as invaluable learning opportunities that engage and promote both personal and intellectual growth.

To further facilitate your learning journey, engage with resources that permit you the flexibility to learn at your own comfort and pace. Many online tutorials integrate interactive elements such as quizzes and exercises designed to reinforce understanding and enhance recall. Books, similar to a hypothetical "AI for Dummies," are designed to break down complex concepts into more manageable segments, rendering them more accessible and digestible to beginners. Additionally, structured courses available on e-learning platforms like Coursera or Udemy offer curated learning paths tailored to cater to various skill levels, providing a step-by-step incremental approach to understanding AI.

Interactive Element: Reflection Exercise

Make it a point to reflect on a time in your life when you embarked on the journey of mastering a new skill that appeared challenging at first glance. What specific strategies or approaches did you employ to overcome the obstacles that arose along the way? How did your confidence and proficiency evolve throughout the journey? Take a moment to jot down your thoughts and utilize these valuable insights to aid and inform your learning journey in AI.

Bear in mind that cultivating technical expertise is not so much about having an all-encompassing knowledge from the onset, but rather about committing to the process of continuous improvement and skill refinement. Your path to acquiring proficiency is uniquely yours, molded and influenced by your personal interests and steadfast determination. By confronting and dispelling fears and misconceptions head-on, you lay a strong and enduring foundation for a fulfilling and enriching experience in both AI and its applications, such as prompt engineering.

Finding Time for Learning in a Busy Schedule

In the whirlwind of daily life, the process of carving out time specifically reserved for learning can indeed feel akin to a Herculean task, akin to the trials of myth and legend. Indeed, the challenge may seem overwhelming at first glance: a daunting enigma interspersed within the chaotic symphony of everyday obligations and responsibilities. Yet, the pursuit of prioritizing learning transcends beyond merely the realm of personal satisfaction—it's a profoundly critical, life-enhancing step toward the grand journey of career advancement and progression. Imagine, if you will, that learning serves as the essential, high-energy fuel that invigorates and powers the complex machine that is your professional trajectory. As industries and sectors continually evolve, transform, and redefine themselves at an unprecedented pace, those who resolutely commit to the noble cause of continuous learning often find themselves impressively ahead of the ever-shifting curve, poised and ready to seize emerging opportunities with confidence and agility. In the dynamic realm of AI and prompt engineering, where change remains a steadfast constant, keeping your skills perennially sharp is not just important; it becomes indispensable. Being adaptable is what renders you not merely employable, but an irreplaceable, vital asset to any organization or endeavor.

Harnessing Time Management Skills

Time management, despite being perceived as a potentially overused and clichéd buzzword, stands as the unwavering backbone of intelligently integrating learning into your daily routine without feeling buried under its weight. Start by deliberately carving out a dedicated learning schedule. However, this doesn't mean you need to clear extensive tracts of time out of your day; even a modest 15 minutes each day can make a substantial difference over time, gradually accumulating to a vast reservoir of knowledge. Identify the times when your mental faculties are at their peak—perhaps during your morning coffee when the world begins to stir yet again or in the quiet solace of the night when tranquility reigns—and make a commitment to stick to it. Set specific, achievable goals for these succinct sessions, such as gaining a deeper understanding of a new AI concept or actively practicing and refining your prompts. This calculated approach not only keeps you on track but also prevents the invaluable pursuit of learning from devolving into an overwhelming chore, thereby making it a more sustainable endeavor.

Utilizing Technology to Enhance Learning

In today's advanced digital age, sophisticated tools and cutting-edge apps are akin to having an astute personal assistant right in your pocket, always at your disposal. They serve as a means of optimizing your valuable time dedicated to learning, ensuring that both efficiency and focus are maintained at the highest standard. A note-taking app like Evernote or OneNote enables you to capture those eureka moments instantly, preserving your insightful reflections for later contemplation. Moreover, a time-tracking tool such as Toggl can diligently monitor your study periods, ensuring that your learning sessions remain both productive and free from the common distractive elements that abound. These tools effectively transform technology from a potential hindrance into a supportive ally on your quest for expanded knowledge and understanding.

Engaging in Incremental Learning

The adoption of incremental learning approaches can completely transform the manner in which you absorb and retain new information. Instead of the age-old method of cramming, consider breaking down learning objectives into smaller, more manageable micro-sessions which statistically improve both retention and understanding. Think of it as snacking on assorted bites of knowledge throughout your day, rather than gorging yourself in a single indulgent session. Actively engaging in daily learning challenges—perhaps tackling a fresh AI concept each day or experimenting with creatively different prompts—keeps the experience fresh and relevant. These bite-sized chunks make it significantly easier to fit learning into the busy tapestry of your life, all while keeping you motivated, engaged, and always coming back for more.

The Strategic Approach to Learning

Incorporating learning into your routine is an endeavor that demands more than just good intentions or sporadic efforts; it requires a strategic approach rooted in commitment and innovation. Prioritizing education isn't about simply finding the time, which may be an elusive endeavor, but rather about consciously making the time and allocating it wisely. With dedication, foresight, and the adoption of tailored strategies, you can weave learning seamlessly into the intricate fabric of your daily life, ensuring that you are perpetually moving forward, continuously growing, and enriching your personal and professional journey, one strategic step at a time.

Building a Supportive Learning Community

Imagine, if you will, having at your disposal an entire ensemble of individuals who are not only knowledgeable about the intricacies of AI and prompt engineering, but also stand as your personal cheerleading squad through every success, big or small, as well as every setback, significant or minor. This truly is the astounding magic that lies in being an active participant within a learning community. Such communities go beyond merely finding people with shared interests; they form spaces where knowledge circulates abundantly, allowing ideas to morph and evolve through collective experiences that are ever-expanding. Networking within these well-knit circles can serendipitously lead to unexpected opportunities that perhaps you hadn't even envisaged before—from unexpected job offers to collaborative projects that stretch the limits of the conceivable. In fact, engaging with a broad spectrum of perspectives not only enriches your understanding but also allows you to approach problems from angles you might not have considered on your own. It's akin to having a personal think tank at your disposal, ready to delve into every conceivable nook and cranny of AI possibilities alongside you, amplifying your endeavors.

Embarking on the journey to find and join such supportive communities might initially seem like a daunting task, but rest assured, it's far easier than it appears. Online forums and discussion groups serve as fantastic starting points that bridge individuals from various backgrounds but with a common interest. Platforms such as Reddit and LinkedIn harbor numerous groups where AI enthusiasts congregate regularly to exchange insights, pose questions, and extend support, creating virtual spaces that function as treasure troves of information. In these forums, you can glean immense value from the experiences of others traversing a similar path. Additionally, local meetups and workshops offer the valuable benefit of face-to-face interaction, which can deepen connections and foster a strong sense of camaraderie. Websites like Meetup.com lay out events organized by interest and location, thus simplifying the process of finding gatherings focused on AI and technology in your area. All that remains is to dive in headfirst, introduce yourself confidently, and refrain from hesitating to pose questions. Keep in mind that every expert once started as a beginner—asking questions is the first step to learning.

Another cornerstone of these communities is the pivotal role of peer support and mentorship in refining and advancing your skills. While embarking on prompt engineering projects, receiving feedback from peers offers perspectives invaluable in refining your approach. Peers, with fresh eyes, can identify subtleties you might have overlooked or suggest alternatives you had not considered. Additionally, cultivating relationships with mentors provides both guidance and accountability. They assist you in setting realistic goals and navigating challenges with newfound confidence. Mentors, having previously walked the same path, can offer sage wisdom from their own experiences and help steer you clear of common pitfalls. Within this reciprocal environment of mutual learning, everyone grows together, thriving off the amplification of shared knowledge and encouragement.

Active participation within these communities is not merely beneficial—it's an essential component of your progress. Engagement transitions you from a passive observer into an active contributor. Share your own successes, challenges, and insights generously with others, as your experiences might provide the missing piece someone else requires to overcome their own hurdles. Engage in collaborative projects to actively apply your learning in real-world situations, which not only enhances your skill set but also cements your reputation as a knowledgeable, reliable community member. Such active involvement fosters mutual benefit and creates an environment where everyone thrives collectively.

In conclusion, a supportive learning community transcends being just a gathering of individuals; it functions as a dynamic ecosystem fueled by shared passion, curiosity, and the collective drive for mutual growth and discovery. By immersing yourself in these vibrant networks, you unlock access to an abundance of resources and perspectives that can accelerate your learning journey and open unforeseen doors. Whether you seek technical advice, require guidance to tackle tough challenges, or are merely looking for encouragement on challenging days, these communities provide a steadfast lifeline, keeping you interconnected, informed, and perpetually inspired.

Addressing Skepticism: The Viability of Making Money with AI

There's a common perception that the excitement surrounding AI is more hype than reality. People often wonder if the skills involved in AI, particularly those in prompt engineering, hold genuine market value. Skepticism isn't uncommon, especially when faced with something that seems too good to be true. It's important to acknowledge these doubts. Many wonder, "Is there really a demand for these skills?" The truth is, while the digital age has undoubtedly made certain tasks easier, it has also created a thirst for new expertise. AI is more than a passing trend; it's reshaping industries and creating countless opportunities for those willing to engage with it.

To counter skepticism, let's look at some hard facts. The AI sector is booming. According to recent studies, there's been a significant increase in AI-related job postings, illustrating a growing demand for these skills. Industries like healthcare, finance, and marketing are actively seeking AI professionals to improve processes and innovate solutions. Furthermore, successful AI startups are cropping up globally, demonstrating the potential for business ventures in this field. Take, for example, startups harnessing AI for personalized healthcare solutions or those revolutionizing e-commerce with advanced customer analytics. These stories aren't just isolated successes; they're evidence of a thriving ecosystem.

Monetization opportunities abound beyond traditional employment. Freelancing and consulting offer avenues for those who prefer independence and flexibility. AI skills are in high demand on platforms like Upwork and Freelancer, where businesses seek expertise to enhance their operations. Additionally, creating and selling AI-driven products or services is a viable path. Whether it's developing an app that simplifies daily tasks or offering AI-based solutions tailored to niche markets, the possibilities are vast. By identifying specific needs and gaps in the market, you can craft products that resonate with consumers and businesses alike.

An entrepreneurial mindset is key to unlocking these opportunities. In every challenge lies the seed of innovation. Viewing obstacles as chances to create something novel can lead to unexpected financial rewards. Identifying niche markets for AI applications can set you apart from competitors. Perhaps there's a local industry that could benefit from automation, or maybe there's a gap in the market for AI tools designed specifically for small businesses. Innovation doesn't always mean reinventing the wheel; sometimes it's about finding a better way to use existing technology.

Adopting an entrepreneurial approach doesn't mean you must start your own company immediately. It could involve collaborating on projects with others or consulting for businesses looking to integrate AI into their operations. By keeping an open mind and staying adaptable, you can uncover opportunities that align with your skills and interests. Remember, the world of AI is still unfolding. As it evolves, so do the ways you can contribute and benefit financially.

The fear of financial instability can deter people from pursuing careers in less traditional fields like AI. However, those who have taken the leap often find themselves in a landscape rich with potential and growth. The journey may seem daunting initially, but the rewards often outweigh the risks. By staying informed about industry trends and continuously honing your skills, you can position yourself strategically in this dynamic field.

Embracing change is part of thriving in the world of AI and prompt engineering. It requires courage to step into unknown territory, but with courage comes opportunity. The ability to adapt and innovate will serve you well as you explore different monetization strategies within this ever-expanding field. It's not just about making money; it's about building a career that excites you and offers limitless possibilities for growth.

The intersection of technology and creativity presents a unique chance to carve out a space for yourself in a rapidly advancing world. The skepticism surrounding AI's financial viability often stems from misunderstanding its potential impact. By exploring various pathways—be it traditional roles, freelance gigs, or entrepreneurial ventures—you open yourself up to experiences that could redefine your career trajectory. As you navigate this exciting landscape, remember that your insights and creativity are invaluable assets waiting to be tapped into for both personal fulfillment and financial success.

Staying Motivated: Setting Goals and Tracking Progress

Imagine embarking on a journey without a map. You'd likely feel lost pretty quickly. That's what it's like trying to learn new skills without setting clear goals. Goals act like a roadmap, guiding you through the learning process and keeping you motivated along the way. Specific, measurable goals can turn abstract desires into tangible milestones. Think of SMART goals—those that are Specific, Measurable, Achievable, Relevant, and Time-bound. These aren't just buzzwords. They're a practical way to break down your objectives into manageable chunks, making the path ahead clearer and less overwhelming.

Once you've set your goals, the next step is keeping track of them. This might sound tedious, but trust me, it's essential. Imagine checking off tasks on a to-do list—there's a sense of accomplishment there, right? That's what tracking does for your learning progress. Digital planners and goal-tracking apps like Todoist or Notion can be invaluable allies here. They help organize your tasks and remind you of upcoming deadlines, ensuring nothing slips through the cracks. Keeping a progress journal also works wonders. It allows you to reflect on your achievements and make adjustments when necessary. This isn't just about ticking boxes; it's about seeing how far you've come and planning your next steps.

Motivation can sometimes wane, especially when challenges arise. But there are ways to keep your spirits high. First, celebrate your milestones. It doesn't matter if they're big or small—acknowledging them reinforces your progress and boosts your confidence. Maybe treat yourself to a nice meal or simply take a moment to pause and reflect on how far you've come. Another tip is to connect your goals with what you truly value. If you're passionate about AI's potential to improve lives, let that drive you when the going gets tough. Aligning your objectives with your personal values can make the process feel more meaningful and rewarding.

Accountability is another powerful motivator. It's easy to slack off when no one's watching, but having someone else in the loop changes everything. Find an accountability partner—a friend, colleague, or mentor—to share your goals with. Regular check-ins will help keep you on track and provide a fresh perspective when you're stuck. These sessions don't have to be formal; a casual chat over coffee or a quick video call can do wonders. It's not just about having someone to report to; it's about knowing someone cares about your progress and wants to see you succeed.

Incorporating these strategies can transform the way you approach learning and skill development. Setting clear goals gives you direction, while tracking ensures you stay on course. Celebrating achievements fuels your motivation, reminding you why you started in the first place. And having someone hold you accountable adds another layer of commitment that can make all the difference. It's a comprehensive approach that not only enhances productivity but also makes the learning journey more enjoyable and fulfilling.

Creating a balance between ambition and reality is crucial here. While it's great to aim high, it's equally important to appreciate where you currently stand. Taking stock of your achievements helps ground you, providing a sense of satisfaction that propels you forward. This balanced perspective fosters resilience, enabling you to navigate setbacks with grace and determination.

In this fast-paced world, staying motivated might seem like an uphill battle at times. But with clear goals, effective tracking systems, and supportive networks in place, you're well-equipped to tackle challenges head-on. Embrace this process, trusting that each step brings you closer to where you want to be—whether it's mastering prompt engineering or exploring new AI frontiers.

Celebrating Small Wins: Building Confidence Gradually

The fast-paced world that we live in often makes us feel as though we should always be leaping from one giant achievement to another, without pause. However, this belief creates an oversight of the smaller, yet immensely important victories we encounter on our path to mastering new skills and achieving our goals. Each small win is like an intrinsic thread that weaves into the larger tapestry of our life's journey. Just like when assembling a puzzle, every single piece you connect provides satisfaction and forward momentum. Completing a tutorial or successfully crafting a single prompt might seem insignificant when compared to the ultimate goal you're striving for, but these are the building blocks of confidence and motivation. By pausing to celebrate these accomplishments, you affirm your efforts and bolster your perseverance, especially when the challenges mount and the path becomes more arduous.

Recognizing Invisible Victories

Amidst the relentless whirl of daily responsibilities, identifying these small wins requires conscious effort. A fruitful method to achieve this is through the art of journaling. At the end of your day, when the dust settles and tranquility returns, spare a few moments to inscribe your triumphs in a journal. No achievement is too trivial to be recorded because this practice helps you shift your attention from tasks left undone to those you conquered. The simple act of rereading your list crystallizes the progress you've made. Additionally, visual progress trackers can serve as vibrant motivators. Imagine adhering a vivacious chart to your wall, one that bursts with color as you hit each milestone. These trackers transform abstract achievements into visible, celebratory artifacts, inches away from transforming into trophies for your mental gallery.

Balancing Big Dreams and Present Growth

In our quest for grand dreams, there lies a significant yet often underestimated power in valuing and appreciating where we stand today. Take a journey through the corridors of your own growth over time. Envision a timeline stretching from the moment you embarked on this journey to the tangible present. In retrospect, gauge the depth of growth, learning, and adaptation you've undergone. This perspective anchors your current achievements in a context of transformation and resilience. You're not merely an echo of the individual who first set foot on this path; you've amassed knowledge and experience, sculpting a version of yourself you should take pride in.

Long-term Benefits and the Confidence Ripple

The foundational confidence built by acknowledging small victories spills over, enhancing every dimension of your life. With growing self-assurance, new challenges lose their daunting guise, revealing themselves instead as fertile grounds for growth and exploration. Problem-solving becomes reinvigorated with creativity and vigor. When you trust in your capabilities, you approach dilemmas with fresh perspectives and initiative. This adaptable mindset is invaluable, particularly in fields like AI and prompt engineering, known for ceaseless transformation.

Strengthening the Foundation of Assurance

Building confidence is akin to meticulously constructing a fortress; it's a gradual process, brick by brick. Every small win you recognize adds a layer of fortitude to the foundation of your self-assuredness, creating a sturdy base capable of supporting future triumphs. Shifting to a mindset wherein challenges are welcomed as opportunities sets you on a path of resilience and readiness. As this outlook becomes ingrained within you, you find unmatched strength to face whatever hurdles emerge ahead.

In conclusion, celebrating small wins nurtures a habit of progress recognition. It's an acknowledgment that every step, irrespective of its magnitude, is indispensable in the grand narrative of your objectives. By internalizing this philosophy, you develop a wellspring of confidence, enriching your journey, ensuring it's both fulfilling and enduring.

As we close this chapter, carry forward the understanding that confidence is not just a result of monumental achievements but accumulates through the appreciation of every success garnered along this journey. Each triumph, no matter how modest, strengthens your stride, fortifying you with the adaptability and resilience you need. With this attitude, you are ready to delve into the subsequent chapter, unraveling how newfound confidence can be harnessed into actionable tactics within AI and prompt engineering.

6

Chapter 5: Enhancing Career Opportunities with Prompt Engineering

Integrating Prompt Engineering into Your Current Job

Imagine arriving at work, coffee in hand, and the day's tasks already streamlined thanks to AI. It's not science fiction; it's the vibrant reality of seamlessly integrating prompt engineering into your role. In the bustling corridors of modern workplaces, where time seems to whiz by and the pressure to deliver quality results swiftly is ever-present, the mantra of working smarter instead of harder takes precedence. So, how do you identify those golden opportunities to elegantly weave AI into the intricate tapestry of your daily grind?

Start your integration journey by meticulously mapping out repetitive tasks. Routine work, such as updating sprawling spreadsheets or responding to an endless stream of similar customer queries, are prime candidates for innovative automation through AI prompts. Consider AI as your ever-attentive digital assistant, poised and ready to take on the mundane spectrum of tasks, liberating your time and energy to concentrate on more invigorating and creative endeavors.

Look at the realm of data analysis too. AI-driven insights have the potential to radically transform how you interpret data, effectively converting what might initially seem like a daunting mountain of numbers into actionable strategies and clear narratives. Imagine receiving a dynamic report that, almost like magic, highlights critical trends and anomalies in real-time, essentially having a seasoned analyst whispering insights into your ear. The inherent beauty of prompt engineering rests in its remarkable ability to enhance decision-making processes. By reducing the manual workload, it frees up indispensable mental space for creative innovation and forecasting. More strategic thinking time could be the pivot between a project that merely meets expectations and one that genuinely exceeds them, leaving a lasting impact.

But how do you introduce AI into your team's workflow without inciting chaos or feelings of unsettlement? The key lies in a gradual infusion. Start with small, manageable steps. Introduce AI tools gradually into team projects. Perhaps you could begin with a pilot project where AI manages data collection or initial analysis phases. This not only showcases the robust capabilities of AI but also builds trust and confidence among team members. Training sessions are key elements of this transition. Organize interactive workshops to meticulously demonstrate efficient prompt usage and encourage open, collaborative discussions. The more comfortable your team becomes with AI, the smoother and more harmonious the integration process will be. Emphasize that AI isn't here to seize control over human endeavors but rather to significantly enhance and augment them.

Consider the story of a marketing professional who courageously embraced prompt engineering for campaign optimization. Before the introduction of AI, they spent countless hours meticulously analyzing past campaigns to painstakingly predict future successes. By integrating AI, they automated this analysis process, allowing for nimble adjustments and more targeted, accurate strategies. The result? An impressive 25% increase in campaign effectiveness and a noticeable boost in team morale. The takeaway here is crystal clear: prompt engineering doesn't merely improve efficiency; it cultivates a fertile environment for innovative thinking and unprecedented success.

Interactive Element: Reflective Exercise

Now, immerse yourself in a moment of introspection. Take a moment to jot down three tasks in your current role that could benefit substantially from AI intervention. Consider both the repetitive, mundane tasks and areas where deeper, insightful data analytics could prove invaluable. Reflect on the potential transformative changes this could bring to your workflow and team dynamics.

The journey of integrating prompt engineering into your job is not merely about adopting new tools; it's about evolving your mindset toward embracing innovative change as an avenue for growth. By astutely identifying areas ripe for AI integration, you're not only bolstering your productivity but also paving the way for dynamic career advancement. Remember, in the ever-evolving world of work, staying ahead of the curve means perpetually staying adaptable. AI is not just a tool; it is a lifelong partner in the journey of innovation, poised and waiting to elevate your career and personal growth to new heights. Through this synergy, you're creating a future where technology and human ingenuity work hand in hand, shaping an exciting landscape of boundless possibilities and prosperous horizons.

Reskilling and Upskilling: Transitioning Careers

Navigating a career shift can feel like standing at the edge of a new adventure, brimming with both excitement and uncertainty. In today's dynamic job market, terms like "reskilling" and "upskilling" pop up frequently, offering pathways for growth and progression. Reskilling involves acquiring new skills to pivot into a different role or industry altogether. Imagine moving from a finance background to a position in AI consultancy. It's about embracing fresh challenges and diversifying your skill set. On the other hand, upskilling focuses on enhancing your existing skills to climb higher within your current field. It's the difference between learning to cook a new cuisine versus perfecting a signature dish. Both paths are about preparing for future successes and adapting to ever-changing demands.

For those looking to transition into prompt engineering, understanding the key skills is crucial. At the heart of this transition lies a robust grasp of AI basics and machine learning principles. These concepts form the backbone of prompt engineering, providing a solid foundation to build upon. Additionally, diving into natural language processing (NLP) is vital. NLP is the bridge that allows computers to understand human language, a fundamental component in crafting effective prompts for AI systems like ChatGPT. Understanding how machines interpret language nuances can give you a significant edge in this field, enabling you to design prompts that elicit precise and contextually relevant responses.

Crafting a roadmap for this career transition involves setting clear objectives and timelines. Start by defining your career goals—whether it's becoming a freelance prompt engineer or securing a role within an innovative tech company. Lay out a timeline with specific milestones, such as completing courses or certifications in AI and NLP. Online platforms like Coursera or Udacity offer specialized courses that cater to both beginners and those seeking advanced knowledge. These courses not only provide formal education but also help you build a network of peers and mentors, essential for navigating your new career path. Certifications can add credibility to your resume, showcasing your commitment to learning and professional growth.

Support systems play a pivotal role in this journey. Online learning platforms offer an array of courses that cater to different learning styles and paces. They provide the flexibility needed to balance learning with current work commitments. Beyond formal education, consider seeking career counseling or joining mentorship programs. Engaging with mentors who have successfully transitioned into prompt engineering can provide invaluable insights and guidance. They can help you navigate challenges, offer advice on skill development, and introduce you to networking opportunities within the AI community.

Transitioning careers, especially into something as cutting-edge as prompt engineering, requires a strategic approach. It's about continuously building your knowledge base while staying attuned to industry trends. The landscape of AI is ever-evolving, with new developments emerging rapidly. Staying informed through industry publications, webinars, and conferences can keep you ahead of the curve, ensuring you're equipped with the latest knowledge and skills. Engage with online AI communities where professionals share their experiences and insights. Platforms like Reddit and LinkedIn host active discussions where you can learn from others' experiences and contribute your own insights.

Embracing reskilling or upskilling is more than just acquiring new knowledge; it's about fostering a mindset of lifelong learning and adaptability. As you enhance your capabilities in AI and prompt engineering, remember that each step forward brings you closer to transforming your career aspirations into reality. Stay curious, be open to change, and don't shy away from opportunities that challenge you to grow beyond your comfort zone. Whether you're starting fresh or building upon existing skills, these efforts are investments in your future success.

Networking and Building Professional Relationships

Networking stands as a cornerstone in the dynamic realm of prompt engineering. It's not just about collecting business cards or adding connections on LinkedIn; it's about forging meaningful relationships that can propel your career forward. Picture this: you're at a tech conference, surrounded by experts and enthusiasts alike. Engaging in conversations here can lead to insights you might never find online. These interactions open doors to industry secrets, emerging trends, and the unlisted job opportunities that everyone covets. Building a solid network within the AI community enhances your reputation, positioning you as a go-to person for collaboration and innovation.

When it comes to networking strategies, it's vital to think both online and offline. Attending industry conferences and events offers direct access to thought leaders and peers. These gatherings provide a platform for learning, sharing ideas, and sparking collaborations. But the digital world is equally crucial. Engaging with AI-focused groups on social media platforms like Twitter or Reddit can connect you with global communities. These virtual spaces foster discussions on the latest AI advancements and prompt engineering techniques, allowing you to stay updated and contribute your insights. By participating actively, you become part of a larger conversation, increasing your visibility and influence.

Professional relationships aren't just about exchanging information; they are about building bridges that lead to career advancement. Collaborations often spring from these connections, offering fresh perspectives and opportunities for innovation. Imagine working on a project with someone you've met through networking—combining your unique skills can lead to groundbreaking results. Moreover, these relationships often blossom into mentorships. A mentor can provide guidance, share experiences, and offer advice that accelerates your professional growth. Being open to mentorship means you're willing to learn from others' paths, avoiding common pitfalls while discovering new opportunities.

Several tools and platforms can facilitate networking efforts effectively. LinkedIn remains a powerful tool for professional connections. It's not just about creating a profile but actively engaging with your network through posts, comments, and messages. Share your thoughts on AI trends or prompt engineering challenges; this not only showcases your expertise but also invites discussions. Meetup is another excellent platform for finding local tech gatherings. Attending these meetups allows you to meet fellow professionals in person, fostering a sense of community that online interactions might lack.

In prompt engineering, networking isn't merely an optional activity—it's a strategic move toward career success. By building strong professional relationships, you gain access to valuable insights and opportunities that can set you apart in the competitive AI landscape. The knowledge shared among peers can spark innovation and inspire new approaches to common challenges. As you nurture these relationships, remember it's a two-way street. Offering support and sharing your expertise enriches the community and strengthens your connections.

Networking also creates pathways for professional development beyond immediate job prospects. The insights gained from these interactions can guide your career trajectory, helping you identify areas for growth and specialization. It's through conversations with industry veterans that you may discover niche markets or emerging technologies ripe for exploration. These insights can lead to strategic career decisions, ensuring you remain adaptable and forward-thinking in an ever-evolving field.

Attending industry events may initially seem daunting, especially if you're new to the scene. However, it's important to approach them with curiosity rather than apprehension. Engage with speakers after sessions, ask questions during panel discussions, and participate in workshops. These actions demonstrate your eagerness to learn and contribute, leaving a positive impression on those you interact with.

Ultimately, the value of networking lies in its ability to expand horizons and foster growth—both personally and professionally. Building these connections enriches your understanding of prompt engineering while offering a support system as you navigate your career path. The relationships formed through networking are often long-lasting, providing ongoing opportunities for collaboration, mentorship, and shared success in the dynamic world of AI.

In the end, remember that networking is not just about what others can do for you; it's about mutual growth and shared success. By cultivating genuine connections within the AI community, you position yourself as an integral part of this exciting and ever-evolving field.

Positioning Yourself as a Prompt Engineering Expert

In a world where AI is rapidly gaining ground, establishing yourself as a prompt engineering expert can put you ahead of the curve. This isn't just about knowing the technical stuff, but about continuous learning and development. The field of AI is ever-evolving, and keeping up with its pace means regularly updating your knowledge. Dive into the latest research articles, attend workshops, and participate in webinars to stay informed. By being proactive in your learning, you not only keep your skills sharp but also position yourself as a knowledgeable resource in your field. Sharing this knowledge is an essential part of building expertise. Consider writing blog posts or contributing articles on platforms like Medium, where you can reach a wider audience interested in AI and prompt engineering. Speaking at events or hosting webinars allows you to share insights directly with peers, further cementing your reputation as a thought leader.

Building a personal brand that reflects your expertise requires intentional effort. Start by creating a personal website or blog that showcases your projects and achievements. This online portfolio acts as a central hub where potential clients or employers can learn about your work and expertise. Highlight successful projects and any notable achievements in prompt engineering. Include detailed case studies that demonstrate how your skills have made a tangible impact. This not only showcases your abilities but also provides proof of your expertise to those considering you for future opportunities. Additionally, keep your LinkedIn profile updated with your latest endeavors, ensuring that it reflects your current focus on prompt engineering.

Public speaking offers another avenue to establish authority in the field. Whether it's speaking at industry conferences or leading webinars, public engagements allow you to share your insights directly with audiences eager to learn. These platforms provide opportunities to discuss the latest trends in AI and prompt engineering, positioning you as a forward-thinking expert. By addressing common challenges and offering solutions, you demonstrate not only your expertise but also your willingness to contribute to the community's growth. Publishing articles on AI and prompt engineering further solidifies your status as a thought leader. Aim to write pieces that are both informative and engaging, offering readers valuable takeaways they can apply in their own work.

Consider the success story of an AI consultant who has built a strong online presence. This individual consistently shares insights on LinkedIn, engages with industry discussions, and publishes articles that explore emerging trends in AI. By maintaining an active online presence, they've positioned themselves as a go-to resource for prompt engineering expertise. This visibility has opened doors to speaking engagements, consulting opportunities, and collaborations with other experts in the field. The key takeaway here is the importance of visibility—showcasing your expertise through various channels amplifies your reach and impact.

To effectively position yourself as an expert, focus on cultivating a unique voice that distinguishes you from others in the field. Share personal anecdotes or experiences that highlight how you've navigated challenges or achieved success in prompt engineering. This not only adds authenticity but also makes your content relatable to others who may be facing similar situations. As you develop your personal brand, remember that consistency is crucial. Regularly update your online presence with fresh content, engage with your network, and seek out new opportunities to showcase your expertise.

Ultimately, positioning yourself as a prompt engineering expert is about more than just technical proficiency. It's about building a reputation as a knowledgeable and reliable resource within the AI community. By continuously learning, sharing insights, and engaging with others in the field, you establish yourself as a thought leader who is not only well-versed in prompt engineering but also committed to advancing the industry. As you embark on this journey of expertise-building, remember that each step forward brings you closer to becoming an influential voice in the world of AI and prompt engineering, opening doors to new opportunities and possibilities along the way.

Case Studies: Career Transformations Through AI

Picture a finance professional, once knee-deep in spreadsheets and quarterly reports, now thriving as an AI consultant. Their career leap wasn't just about switching industries; it was a bold move into the future. This shift hinged on leveraging skills honed over years—critical analysis, problem-solving, and strategic thinking—now applied to AI solutions. These transferable skills became their assets, guiding businesses toward smarter solutions. In consultancy, their financial acumen became invaluable, helping clients navigate the economic implications of adopting AI technologies. Embracing AI didn't mean discarding past experiences; it was about evolving them into new contexts.

Consider another transformation: a dedicated teacher stepping into educational technology. Initially focused on classroom instruction, they embraced AI to enhance learning experiences. Their understanding of pedagogy and curriculum development turned into a foundation for creating adaptive learning platforms. By integrating AI, they crafted personalized educational experiences that catered to diverse learning styles, improving student engagement and outcomes. Their journey highlights the power of embracing continuous learning and adaptation. In this new role, they not only impacted individual students but also influenced how education systems approached technology integration.

The success stories of these individuals illuminate key factors behind successful transformations. Leveraging transferable skills stands out as a significant advantage. Skills honed in one field often find valuable applications in another, especially when combined with AI's capabilities. This adaptability is crucial in today's dynamic job market, where industries are constantly evolving. Continuous learning and adaptation emerge as indispensable traits. Staying updated with AI advancements and industry trends ensures professionals remain relevant and equipped to tackle new challenges.

In analyzing these transformations, certain lessons and best practices become clear. Networking and mentorship play pivotal roles in navigating career changes. Building connections within the AI community provides insights and opens doors to opportunities that might otherwise remain hidden. Mentors offer guidance, share experiences, and provide support during transitions. Adapting to industry trends and demands is equally critical. Understanding where the industry is headed allows professionals to align their skills and initiatives with emerging needs, positioning themselves as valuable assets in their new roles.

Real-world examples of overcoming challenges and achieving success can be powerful motivators for those considering career changes. Consider the story of an individual who faced skepticism when transitioning from a traditional role to AI consultancy. Initially met with doubts about their ability to grasp new technologies, they turned these challenges into opportunities for growth. By immersing themselves in AI courses and seeking mentorship, they not only developed technical expertise but also gained confidence in their abilities. Their resilience paid off as they secured a position that allowed them to shape AI-driven strategies for companies across various sectors.

Another inspiring example involves a teacher who encountered resistance when advocating for technology integration in schools. Undeterred, they pursued additional training in educational technology and collaborated with like-minded educators to showcase the benefits of AI in classrooms. Their persistence led to the successful implementation of AI tools that transformed learning environments, proving that innovation often requires perseverance and vision.

These case studies remind us that career transformations are not just about changing jobs; they're about evolving identities and embracing new challenges. Leveraging past experiences, embracing continuous learning, and staying adaptable are key components of successful transitions. Networking, mentorship, and aligning with industry trends further enhance the journey from one career path to another.

In contemplating your own career transformation journey, draw inspiration from these real-world examples. Recognize the skills you've developed over time and explore how they can be applied in new contexts. Embrace challenges as opportunities for growth, and seek guidance from mentors who have navigated similar paths. Remember that each step forward is a chance to redefine your professional identity and contribute meaningfully to the evolving landscape of AI and prompt engineering.

Strategic Career Planning with AI Skills

Strategic career planning is like charting a course on a map where AI skills serve as your compass. As the world of work evolves at a dizzying pace, aligning your career goals with industry trends becomes crucial. This isn't just about staying relevant; it's about anticipating the future and positioning yourself accordingly. Think of it like surfing: you want to catch the wave before it crests. By understanding where AI is heading, you can set your sights on skills that will be in demand, ensuring you ride smoothly through the swells of technological change.

To effectively navigate your career path, a structured approach is crucial. Start by setting clear, tangible objectives. Short-term goals can be as simple as mastering a new AI tool or completing a relevant course. Long-term aspirations might include transitioning into a leadership role or pioneering a new AI application within your industry. Identifying potential career paths requires you to look both inward and outward. Consider your passions and strengths, then align them with opportunities in the AI landscape. Keep an eye on emerging roles and industries; AI's reach is vast and extends into areas you might not have considered, from healthcare to creative arts.

Continuous learning isn't just a buzzword; it's a necessity in strategic career planning. The AI field is like a fast-flowing river, constantly changing with new developments and innovations. Staying put isn't an option if you want to keep pace. Make it a habit to regularly update your knowledge and skills. Attend workshops, read industry reports, and engage in online courses that pique your interest. This proactive approach not only sharpens your expertise but also keeps you adaptable to whatever the future holds. Remember, in this digital age, learning doesn't stop when you leave the classroom; it's a lifelong commitment.

As you navigate these waters, resources become your lifebuoys, keeping you afloat and guiding you toward your destination. Career assessment tools are invaluable for gaining insights into your strengths and weaknesses. They help you identify areas where your skills align with market demands and where there might be gaps to fill. Workshops offer hands-on experiences that deepen your understanding of AI applications in real-world scenarios. Additionally, regularly reviewing AI industry reports and forecasts can provide a macro-level view of where opportunities lie. These insights allow you to make informed decisions about where to focus your efforts.

In strategic planning, awareness of broader trends is vital. AI is transforming industries at a staggering rate, creating new roles and reshaping old ones. By keeping abreast of these shifts, you can position yourself at the forefront of innovation rather than scrambling to catch up. This strategic foresight allows you to anticipate which skills will be valued in the future and prepare accordingly. It's about being proactive rather than reactive, ensuring that when opportunities arise, you're ready to seize them with both hands.

As we conclude this chapter, remember that strategic career planning with AI skills isn't about following a rigid path; it's about adaptability and foresight. You've explored how aligning with industry trends, setting clear goals, committing to continuous learning, and utilizing resources can place you ahead in the game. It's about crafting a career that not only survives but thrives in the evolving landscape of AI. The next chapter will delve into practical applications of these strategies, showcasing how they translate into real-world success stories and tangible outcomes. Stay tuned as we explore how these principles come alive in the vibrant world of prompt engineering and beyond.

7

Chapter 6: Staying Current and Innovative

Keeping Up with the Latest AI Developments

Imagine waking up to discover that your smartphone, almost mimicking a clairvoyant, predicts your daily itinerary, your meals, and even your mood swings before you even reach for it. This scenario, which might seem like something plucked straight out of the pages of a science fiction novel, is swiftly becoming a tangible reality as artificial intelligence (AI) advances by leaps and bounds. In a world where AI is continuously evolving at almost an exponential rate, staying informed isn't just beneficial—it's essential for anyone who wishes to remain relevant and seize the myriad opportunities arising in this dynamic sector. The speed at which these technologies advance is truly astonishing; what appears to be the pinnacle of innovation today could very well become obsolete within the span of a few months as new discoveries and enhancements redefine the landscape of interaction between humans and technology. Groundbreaking research doesn't only polish existing applications; it serves as a key to unlock doors that lead to unprecedented possibilities, previously unimagined in this vast universe of AI possibilities.

But how does one stay updated and in sync with these incessant changes? Firstly, identifying a range of trustworthy and reputable sources is absolutely crucial. Academic journals, for instance, are akin to hidden treasure troves, filled with cutting-edge research and insight in AI and machine learning that almost sparkle with innovation and fresh ideas. They delve deep, offering insights into the latest findings and theoretical advancements that push the boundaries of what's possible today. In parallel, reliable AI news outlets like MIT News act as a filter, providing a digestible snapshot of industry trends, breakthroughs, and potential technological disruptions. Consulting these sources ensures that you're not merely consuming bullet points of information, but rather becoming well-founded in knowledgeable insights backed by rigorous research and thorough analysis. Developing the ability to sift through and discern credible information amid the cacophony of noise and misinformation is a skill of immense value in this rapidly evolving domain.

Networking extends beyond exchanging pleasantries and plays a pivotal role in the information-gathering process. Engaging directly with professionals working within the AI field can yield firsthand insights into the latest trends, innovations, and potential game-changers. Attending AI conferences and summits can prove particularly invaluable; these gatherings bring the crème de la crème of the industry together, where experts eagerly share their experiences, predictions, and visions, offering you a direct line to the pulsating heartbeat of AI innovation. In networking, the goal transcends just collecting business cards or establishing superficial connections; it's about cultivating relationships that genuinely enrich your understanding, spark new ideas, and maybe even lead to collaborative ventures down the line.

Achieving efficiency in information consumption has become something akin to an art form. By carefully curating a personalized news feed tailored specifically to your interests, you can streamline this process significantly. Employ modern tools like Feedly or Flipboard to aggregate content from your favored AI publications and blogs, ensuring you're not just inundated with information, but instead receiving curated updates that align with your personal interests and professional goals. Employ a strategy of setting aside dedicated time slots for reading and analysis to ensure that you're engaging deeply with the material, not just skimming headlines. Consider integrating time blocks into your weekly schedule where you proactively dive into new articles or unravel research papers, allowing you to internalize and weave new knowledge thoughtfully into your existing expertise.

Interactive Element: Building Your Information Network

Take a moment to identify and list three reputable AI sources you have encountered or are eager to explore further. Consider how you can seamlessly incorporate these into your weekly routine—perhaps through subscribing to insightful newsletters or joining engaging online forums teeming with vibrant discussions on AI topics. Reflect on which professional networks or events could significantly enhance your learning horizon and keep you intellectually connected to the latest developments and avant-garde trends in AI.

Embracing these strategies doesn't just keep you informed— it effectively positions you as an agile thinker, adept at adapting to the waves of change that continually sweep through the industry. As you navigate this fascinating and ever-evolving landscape of AI, remember that staying current transcends mere absorption of information; it's about processing, applying, and creatively integrating it into your work. By keeping pace with advancements, you don't just enhance your skill set; you position yourself as a pioneering, forward-thinking professional, poised to lead and spur innovation in AI-driven environments for tomorrow and beyond.

Exploring Emerging Tools and Technologies

Picture this: you're sipping your morning coffee, and with just a few taps on your device, you're generating reports, crafting narratives, and even creating music. This isn't a far-off dream but a daily reality shaped by cutting-edge AI tools. One standout is the rise of natural language generation APIs. These tools transform how we interact with data and information, allowing for seamless conversion of structured data into human-readable text. Imagine using an API that can take your sales data and generate a comprehensive business report in minutes. It's like having a personal assistant who never tires, always ready to synthesize information with precision and flair.

Alongside these APIs, AI-powered data analytics platforms are making waves. They're like having a backstage pass to the inner workings of complex datasets. These platforms don't just crunch numbers; they interpret them, offering insights that can drive strategic decisions faster than ever before. They allow businesses to pinpoint trends, foresee market shifts, and tailor strategies with unprecedented accuracy. The potential doesn't stop there. These platforms enable real-time data analysis, making them indispensable in industries where time is of the essence.

But what happens when you blend AI with augmented reality? Magic, that's what. Integrating augmented reality with AI opens up a realm of possibilities. Imagine walking through a virtual store where AI anticipates your preferences, offering suggestions as you browse. It's a personalized shopping experience that's not just futuristic but transformative. And let's not forget blockchain's role in secure AI transactions. By ensuring transparency and security, blockchain adds a layer of trust that enhances AI transactions, making them not only faster but also more reliable.

These technologies are not just reshaping workflows; they're redefining market dynamics and consumer expectations. People now crave personalized experiences that cater to their unique preferences. AI tools that deliver tailored interactions are no longer optional—they're expected. This shift is influencing industry trends, pushing businesses to innovate or risk becoming obsolete. Personalized AI experiences are becoming the norm, not the exception.

So how do you keep up with all these innovations? Early adoption is key, but it requires careful consideration. Start by pilot testing new AI tools in controlled settings. This allows you to gauge their impact without committing fully. Assessing ROI is crucial here—ensure that the benefits outweigh the costs before moving forward. Scalability is another factor to consider. A tool might work wonders on a small scale, but can it handle larger operations? Evaluate its scalability before integrating it into your workflow.

Early adoption also involves staying open to experimentation. Not every tool will be a perfect fit, and that's okay. The goal is to explore new possibilities and see what works best for you and your team. This process requires flexibility and adaptability—qualities that are invaluable in the ever-evolving landscape of AI technology.

The journey through these emerging tools is both thrilling and daunting. It's a dance between innovation and practicality, where each step forward opens new doors and possibilities. As you navigate this landscape, remember that staying informed and adaptable is your greatest ally.

Continuous learning remains paramount in this fast-paced environment. It's the fuel that keeps your curiosity alive and your skills sharp. Embrace online courses, webinars, and workshops as opportunities to gain fresh perspectives and insights. These platforms provide access to industry experts who can offer guidance and inspiration as you explore new technologies.

Collaboration plays an essential role too. By working with others, you can leverage diverse perspectives and ideas, leading to innovative solutions you might not have considered on your own. Whether through cross-disciplinary teams or partnerships between tech companies and creative industries, collaboration fosters creativity and drives progress.

Building a reputation as an innovator in AI is within reach if you embrace these strategies. Share your projects publicly, engage with AI communities, and contribute original ideas that push the boundaries of what's possible. Establishing yourself as an innovator enhances your career opportunities and positions you as a thought leader in the field.

You're on the cusp of an exciting frontier where technology meets creativity. It's a space where imagination knows no bounds, limited only by your willingness to explore and experiment. As you delve into these emerging tools and technologies, remember that innovation isn't just about what you create; it's about how you approach challenges and seize opportunities with open arms and an open mind.

Continuous Learning: Courses, Webinars, and Beyond

In the fast-paced world of AI, the need for continuous learning is undeniable. Think of it as a never-ending adventure, where each new discovery paves the way for another. Staying competitive here means keeping your skills sharp and your knowledge up-to-date. As technology races ahead, those who rest on their laurels risk being left behind. The rapid pace of AI development means that what you know today might be old news tomorrow. Embracing lifelong learning isn't just beneficial—it's crucial for anyone looking to thrive in this field. It's about building a toolkit that evolves with the times, ensuring you're always ready to tackle whatever challenges or opportunities come your way.

For those seeking to expand their knowledge, the world is brimming with resources. Online platforms like Coursera, edX, and Udacity offer a treasure trove of courses tailored to AI enthusiasts at every level. These platforms host classes from renowned institutions, making high-quality education accessible to all. Additionally, AI-specific certification programs provide a more structured path. They offer credentials that can boost your resume and signal your expertise in a competitive job market. Whether you're just starting out or looking to enhance your skills, these resources can be invaluable. They allow you to learn at your own pace, fitting education into your schedule in a way that works for you.

Webinars and workshops add another layer to your learning arsenal. These formats are interactive by nature, offering opportunities to engage with industry experts and thought leaders directly. It's not just about absorbing information—it's about participating in discussions, asking questions, and gaining insights from those at the forefront of AI innovation. Attending these events can provide you with unique perspectives that you won't find in textbooks or online courses. Moreover, they often foster networking opportunities, allowing you to connect with like-minded individuals who share your passion for AI.

Balancing continuous learning with life's other demands can be tricky, but it's certainly doable with the right strategies. Start by setting aside dedicated time for learning each week. This could be as simple as blocking off an hour on Sunday mornings or dedicating your lunch break on Wednesdays to catching up on the latest AI research. Incorporating micro-learning sessions into your daily routine can also make a big difference. These short bursts of focused study—whether it's watching a quick video tutorial or reading an article—can fit seamlessly into even the busiest of schedules.

To maximize burstiness and perplexity in your learning process, diversify your sources and formats. Don't just stick to one type of resource; mix it up between courses, webinars, articles, and podcasts. This variety keeps things fresh and exciting, preventing burnout and keeping you engaged. Implement techniques like stemming and lemmatization when tackling dense materials—break down complex topics into manageable pieces to enhance comprehension and retention.

Think about adjusting your approach based on Zipf's law—focus more on the frequently used concepts and terms in AI while occasionally diving into less common ones to broaden your understanding. This strategy ensures a balanced acquisition of knowledge, where you're well-versed in core principles but also aware of niche areas that might offer unique insights.

Engage with the community by joining forums or participating in online discussions about recent AI developments or challenges you've encountered. Sharing your experiences and learning from others can deepen your understanding and reinforce what you've learned. It's also an excellent way to build connections with peers who may become collaborators or mentors down the line.

Remember, continuous learning isn't just about acquiring new information—it's about developing a mindset that embraces change and seeks out growth opportunities. By integrating these strategies into your daily life, you'll not only stay current with AI advancements but also cultivate the adaptability needed to thrive in an ever-evolving landscape.

Innovating with AI: Encouraging Creative Applications

Innovation in AI isn't just about what you create; it's about how you think. Cultivating a creative mindset is the first step toward groundbreaking applications. Embrace experimentation with open arms. Allow yourself to make bold moves and take risks, even if it means stumbling along the way. Each misstep is a learning opportunity that can guide you to unexpected discoveries. Encourage a culture of curiosity where asking "what if" leads to exploring uncharted territories. Diverse perspectives fuel creativity—invite ideas from different fields and backgrounds to enrich your projects. Diversity isn't just about ticking boxes; it's about bringing fresh viewpoints that challenge the status quo.

The creative potential of AI stretches across various sectors, weaving its magic in unexpected ways. Picture an AI composing symphonies that evoke emotions or crafting visual art that captures the essence of human experience. These aren't just novelties; they're redefining what creativity means in a tech-driven world. Consider the realm of storytelling, where AI-driven narratives offer twists and turns crafted by algorithms. This fusion of technology and creativity pushes boundaries, offering experiences that are as unique as they are engaging. In fields like marketing, AI's ability to generate innovative campaigns demonstrates its potential to transform how we connect with audiences.

To nurture innovation, consider adopting frameworks like design thinking—a methodology that encourages empathy and experimentation. Start with understanding the user's needs, then move on to ideation, where wild ideas are not only welcome but encouraged. Prototyping and testing allow you to refine these concepts, ensuring they solve real-world problems effectively. This approach isn't limited to product development; it's a mindset that can be applied to any aspect of AI work, inspiring solutions that might otherwise remain hidden. Encourage your team or peers to engage with these processes, fostering an environment where creativity thrives.

Collaboration acts as a catalyst for innovation, magnifying ideas into transformative solutions. Cross-disciplinary teams bring together diverse expertise, sparking new insights that may not emerge in homogenous groups. Imagine an AI project where tech experts work alongside creatives, each contributing their unique skills to a shared vision. This collaborative spirit doesn't just result in better outcomes; it builds a culture of mutual respect and learning. Partnerships between tech companies and creative industries offer fertile ground for innovation. By leveraging their strengths, they create products and experiences that push the envelope of what's possible.

The journey toward innovation is deeply personal yet profoundly collective. It's a dance between individual inspiration and collaborative synergy. As you explore AI's potential, remember that creativity isn't confined to traditional boundaries—it's an ever-expanding field where imagination meets possibility. Encourage those around you to embrace this mindset, fostering an environment where innovation becomes not just an aspiration but a way of life.

Visual Element: Mind Map for Creative Exploration

Create a mind map centered around a specific problem or goal you'd like AI to address in your work or personal projects. Branch out with ideas on how AI can be applied creatively to solve this problem or achieve this goal. Use colors and images to represent different concepts and connections, encouraging free-flowing thought and visual brainstorming.

Through this lens of creativity, AI becomes more than a tool—it becomes a partner in innovation, capable of inspiring new ways of thinking and doing. Whether you're crafting narratives or developing business strategies, let your imagination run wild as you explore the intersections between technology and human ingenuity.

Building a Reputation as an Innovator in AI

Imagine walking into a room where everyone knows your name, not because of some lucky break, but because you've carved out a niche as an innovator in AI. Being recognized as a trailblazer comes with perks—doors open, opportunities abound, and your insights carry weight. Your visibility in the AI community skyrockets, drawing attention from peers and industry leaders alike. People seek your opinions, valuing your perspective in shaping the future of AI. This elevated status doesn't just enhance your career prospects; it positions you as a thought leader capable of influencing change and driving progress. Leadership roles often follow, granting you the platform to shape AI's narrative and contribute meaningfully to the field's evolution.

Building this reputation requires more than just skill—it demands a strategic approach to personal branding. Sharing your innovative projects and ideas publicly can set you apart. Whether it's through blog posts, social media updates, or video content, showcasing your work highlights your unique contributions to the field. Engaging actively with AI communities and forums further cements your presence. Participating in discussions, offering insights, and collaborating on projects demonstrate your commitment to advancing the field. This engagement is not about self-promotion—it's about contributing to a larger conversation and building relationships that enrich both you and the community.

Your reputation as an innovator hinges on thought leadership. Contributing original ideas and insights establishes your authority in the field. Publishing research papers or articles allows you to share your findings and perspectives with a broader audience. These publications serve as a testament to your expertise, demonstrating your ability to think critically and creatively about AI's challenges and opportunities. Presenting at conferences and seminars amplifies your voice even further. These platforms provide the chance to engage with other experts, exchange ideas, and inspire others with your vision for AI's future.

Consider the path of successful innovators like Andrew Ng, co-founder of Coursera and an AI pioneer. His work in deep learning and online education has left an indelible mark on the industry. Ng's emphasis on accessible education has empowered countless learners worldwide, showcasing how innovative thinking can transform lives. Similarly, Fei-Fei Li, a professor at Stanford University, has been instrumental in advancing computer vision research. Her efforts in democratizing AI education reflect a commitment to fostering diversity and inclusivity within the field. These individuals exemplify how innovation goes beyond technical prowess—it involves a passion for progress and a drive to make meaningful contributions.

Organizations like OpenAI also exemplify innovation at scale. Their commitment to developing safe and beneficial AI serves as a beacon for responsible innovation. By prioritizing transparency and ethical considerations, they've set a standard for how AI can be leveraged for societal good. OpenAI's work underscores that innovation isn't just about pushing technological boundaries—it's about ensuring those advancements align with ethical values and benefit humanity as a whole.

As you embark on this path toward building a reputation as an innovator, remember that it's not solely about personal accolades. It's about creating value for others and contributing positively to the AI community. Share your successes and failures openly; transparency fosters trust and encourages collaboration. Embrace curiosity as a driving force—ask questions, challenge assumptions, and explore new possibilities without fear of failure.

Mentorship plays a pivotal role here too. Seek guidance from those who have walked this path before you while offering support to those just starting out. Sharing knowledge fosters a culture of learning and growth within the community.

Ultimately, building a reputation as an innovator requires a blend of creativity, dedication, and humility. It's about striving for excellence while remaining grounded in the values that drive progress forward. As you navigate this journey toward innovation and recognition in AI, let your passion guide you—it's the spark that fuels transformation and shapes the world of tomorrow.

The Future of Prompt Engineering: Trends to Watch

Imagine a world where AI isn't just a tool we use sporadically, but an intrinsic and indispensable component of our everyday existence. The trajectory of prompt engineering is unmistakably moving towards this future, where AI becomes deeply interwoven into every facet of our daily routines and interactions. Picture smart homes that don't just react, but actually anticipate your needs and desires, intuitively adjusting the lighting, temperature, and even music to match your moods and routines. Consider virtual assistants, not bound by mere functional commands, but enriched with the capacity to grasp and cater to your unique preferences and habits, ultimately crafting an environment that feels tailor-made. This seamless integration of AI is a vision centered not only on convenience but also on creating highly personalized experiences that effectively enhance both individual efficiency and personal satisfaction. As AI's capabilities advance, it transcends the realm of task management, evolving into a sophisticated entity that comprehends and interprets human nuances more effectively, rendering everyday interactions deeply personalized and increasingly meaningful.

Ethical and Transparent AI Practices

With the burgeoning landscape of personalized AI interactions, we are on the cusp of a transformative shift towards ethical and transparent AI practices. This critical change stems from a heightened awareness and understanding of AI's profound societal impact. Today's AI practitioners are keenly focused on constructing systems that are impressively functional and impactful, yet simultaneously fair, unbiased, and equitable. By prioritizing transparency, developers empower users to gain insights into the underlying mechanics of AI decision-making processes. This approach is vital in fostering a trusting, accountable relationship between the technology and its users. The shift toward ethical AI is reconfiguring industries on a broad scale, influencing everything from recruitment and hiring processes to customer service frameworks, as organizations endeavor to create systems that serve and benefit all stakeholders equitably.

The implications of these forward-looking trends are far-reaching and significant. For instance, in the critical domain of healthcare, personalized AI has the potential to revolutionize patient care paradigms. It enables the delivery of bespoke treatment plans and enhances diagnostic accuracy, ensuring that patient care is no longer a one-size-fits-all approach but rather a highly customized service reflecting the intricacies of individual patient needs. In the sphere of education, adaptive learning platforms emerge as transformative tools, capable of customizing lessons to accommodate and benefit diverse learning styles, thereby boosting both engagement and academic outcomes. For AI practitioners, these trends open the door to boundless opportunities for innovation and advancement. There exists a burgeoning demand for AI-powered creative tools poised to redefine the realms of art, music, and literature production. Concurrently, the market for AI-driven personalization services is expanding, as businesses seek innovative strategies to offer unique and resonant experiences to their audiences.

To effectively capitalize on these burgeoning opportunities, flexibility must be woven into workflows and strategies. Embrace the inevitability of change by maintaining an openness to new ideas and innovative approaches. Adaptability transforms into an essential ally as we navigate the ever-evolving technological landscape. Investing in continuous learning is equally paramount; remaining updated on the latest developments not only ensures competitiveness but also fosters the ability to leverage emerging trends effectively. Engaging in workshops and courses that delve into the intricate intersection of AI and ethical considerations becomes vital, as an understanding of these concepts will play a pivotal role in steering the future technological landscape.

Fostering Innovation and Collaboration

Preparing for future technological advancements also requires cultivating a vibrant culture of innovation within teams and organizations. Encourage bold experimentation and support creative endeavors that dare to push boundaries and challenge the status quo. This innovative mindset not only drives technological progress but also empowers individuals to contribute their unique perspectives and talents toward shared objectives. Collaboration emerges as a fundamental element in this context; working collectively amplifies creativity, facilitating the development of solutions that may not be conceived in isolation.

In conclusion, the future of prompt engineering is filled with promise and potential. As AI becomes more deeply integrated into our lives, the landscape is replete with opportunities for growth and innovation. By steadfastly embracing ethical practices and championing personalization, we have the opportunity to shape a future where technology meaningfully enhances the human experience. As we look forward, remember that flexibility and continuous learning remain pivotal tools for successfully adapting to the challenges and changes that lie ahead. In the following chapter, we'll delve into the practical application of these principles across diverse sectors, unlocking new possibilities for creativity and collaboration in the dynamic world of AI.

Curating a Comprehensive Resource List

Imagine standing in front of an expansive library, enveloped by the distinctive scent of old and new pages mingling as each tome silently promises a journey of discovery. Each book you encounter represents a gateway to new knowledge, inviting you to dive deeper into the intricate world of prompt engineering and Artificial Intelligence (AI). Much like a well-curated library, a thoroughly organized resource list serves as a trove of insights, offering guidance and direction as you navigate the broad expanse of this ever-evolving field. As you embark on this intellectual voyage, having access to an array of learning materials becomes an indispensable asset in your pursuit of mastery.

Let's begin by spotlighting some indispensable texts and resources that serve as the keystones of AI understanding. Central to your exploration should be "Artificial Intelligence: A Guide to Intelligent Systems" by Michael Negnevitsky. This seminal work acts as a fundamental pillar, meticulously constructed to provide crystal clear elucidations and relatable, real-world applications of AI principles. Moreover, to augment the knowledge gleaned from traditional texts, consider delving into AI-oriented Massive Open Online Courses (MOOCs) available on platforms like edX and Coursera. These courses offer structured learning pathways that cater to a spectrum of skills and aptitudes, ensuring that whether you're a novice or a seasoned practitioner, you're equipped with the knowledge to succeed.

To truly immerse yourself in the realm of AI, it's important to explore an array of media formats. Cognizant of the fact that people assimilate information at varied paces and through differing modalities, contemplate incorporating alternative media into your learning regimen. For instance, many individuals find auditory and visual learning more engaging and impactful. Hence, the "AI Alignment Podcast" by the Future of Life Institute becomes a valuable resource, offering deep dives into the ethical quandaries and prospective paths of AI advancement. Simultaneously, video series like "Two Minute Papers" on YouTube distill complex subjects into easily digestible snippets, perfect for those seeking a swift but substantial intake of knowledge during a quick morning coffee break.

In curating a resource list aimed at catering to an eclectic array of skill levels, consider the needs of both the novice and the experienced learner. For beginners, there's "What is AI?" by CrashCourse on YouTube—it provides a gentle, yet comprehensive introduction, ensuring newcomers aren't flung into the depths without preparation. Conversely, for those who possess a deeper grounding in the field, absorbing cutting-edge articles from AI conferences may prove enlightening. These peer-reviewed papers serve as a gateway to the forefront of AI research and innovative methodologies, offering intriguing insights into the rapidly evolving landscape of AI technology and theories.

Being able to effectively utilize these resources necessitates the establishment of clear learning objectives. It is important to ask yourself: What are your aspirations with each book, article, or course? Are you aiming to secure a holistic understanding of AI, or do you harbor a desire to specialize in a niche segment of this vast domain? Defining these objectives not only guides your study sessions but also ensures that each resource you engage with serves a distinct purpose and contributes tangibly to your personal growth and expertise. Moreover, applying newfound knowledge to practical projects as you accrue it is a crucial, hands-on methodology to reinforce concepts. By engaging in this practice, you will find your comprehension significantly bolstered and retention enhanced for long-term success.

Interactive Element: Resource Utilization Checklist

As part of this expansive learning endeavor, create a meticulously organized checklist to streamline your educational process. Incorporate columns for resource names, designated skill levels, intended learning goals, and course or book completion status. This pragmatic tool serves to track your progress diligently, ensuring you maintain a diversified and comprehensive learning journey.

Engaging with these broad-ranging resources through a systematic routine can fundamentally elevate your understanding of AI and prompt engineering. By exploring an array of media formats and tailoring your educational experiences to your existing skill level, you'll find yourself not only more knowledgeable but also more assured and adept in the application of these learned skills. Whether you're flipping the pages of a cornerstone text over your morning coffee, or tuning into a thought-provoking podcast during a leisurely commute, each fragment of information becomes an integral component of a broader tapestry. These elements interlock, ultimately forming a comprehensive picture of AI's vast potential, empowering you to transcend mere understanding and move towards impactful application in the field.

Engaging with Online Communities and Forums

Finding your tribe within the expansive and dynamic landscape of Artificial Intelligence (AI) is akin to discovering a hidden gem in a vast, enchanted garden. These online communities serve as vibrant arenas where AI enthusiasts and seasoned professionals seamlessly blend their varied experiences and abundant knowledge. Picture these spaces as lively marketplaces brimming with a plethora of ideas, a place where the brilliance of collaboration blooms through the exchange of insights with fellow aficionados. Among the most energetic and bustling hubs are platforms like Reddit, featuring forums such as r/MachineLearning and r/ArtificialIntelligence. These forums are constantly humming with activity and offer a persistent stream of thought-provoking discussions about the latest trends, formidable challenges, and groundbreaking breakthroughs within the AI landscape. Similarly, Stack Exchange stands as an invaluable repository of knowledge, an oasis for those who seek answers to the often-intricate queries related to AI, making it a vital resource for both burgeoning learners and seasoned experts.

There are manifold benefits to immersing oneself in these communities and becoming an engaged participant. They serve as invaluable platforms for showcasing one's projects and receiving constructive feedback from a global cohort of like-minded peers. Imagine, for a moment, presenting your meticulously crafted AI model to this diverse audience and receiving nuanced insights and perspectives from someone situated halfway around the globe. This kind of peer feedback is crucial, serving as a cornerstone for refining your work and honing your skills. Furthermore, community-driven events, often exclusively available to members, unlock a treasure trove of networking opportunities that might otherwise remain obscured or elusive. Whether it manifests as an online hackathon, a thought-provoking seminar, or an engaging webinar, these events foster meaningful connections that have the potential to be pivotal along your career journey.

Cultivating Active Participation

To truly thrive in these forums, mere lurking in the digital shadows simply won't suffice. Flourishing in these spaces demands being an active and visible contributor, one who cultivates a reputation for thoughtful and insightful engagement. Begin by posing intelligent questions that ignite lively discussions, and offer answers that add substantial value to ongoing conversations. When you share your personal experiences or gleanings from AI experiments, you enrich the community with a treasure trove of unique perspectives. This habit of contributing meaningfully not only amplifies your visibility but also establishes you as a reliable and respected voice within the community. Your journey towards becoming a trusted contributor is marked by your willingness to engage meaningfully, always seeking not just to receive, but to give generously.

Collaborative Opportunities

The opportunities for collaboration and learning in these dynamic spaces are indeed vast. Community-led AI challenges serve as beacons for teamwork, enabling you to tackle complex problems collaboratively alongside individuals who bring diverse skills and perspectives to the metaphorical table. These collaborative projects often yield innovative solutions that may have remained elusive if pursued in solitary endeavors. Group study sessions for AI courses offer another excellent avenue for learning collaboratively, providing both mutual support and motivation as you and your peers grapple with the intricacies of challenging concepts together. These sessions serve not only as academic endeavors but also as communal experiences that enrich your learning journey.

Broader Impacts and Benefits of Participation

Engaging with online communities transcends the simple act of information gathering; it is about actively participating in the larger conversation that surrounds AI. It is within these spaces that you will find boundless inspiration, genuine camaraderie, and unwavering support as you navigate the complex terrain of prompt engineering and AI. The connections and friendships you forge here can open doors to unexpected opportunities, ranging from collaborative projects that ignite new ideas to potential career advancements that propel you forward. Whether you're contributing insightful commentary on the latest AI model, diving into a spirited group challenge, or celebrating the small victories along the way, these interactions become invaluable stepping stones on your path toward both personal growth and professional development. Thus, the journey of engaging with these online communities is a holistic one, offering not just knowledge and skills, but also a profound sense of belonging and purpose within the vast world of AI.

Participating in AI and Prompt Engineering Challenges

Envision yourself stepping onto a grand stage, buzzing with the electricity of intellect and ambition, where countless brilliant minds gather, each motivated by the quest to tackle some of the most engaging and sophisticated puzzles crafted by mankind. This vivid imagery encapsulates the essence of engaging in artificial intelligence (AI) challenges—a vibrant and fiercely competitive arena where innovation, creativity, and the unwavering thirst for knowledge are the revered currencies of success. These challenges embody more than the mere pursuit of victory; indeed, they serve as invaluable platforms for honing one's skills and acquiring intricate, tangible experiences. By immersing yourself in these environments, you are positioned in real-world problem-solving scenarios, tasked with rigorously testing and refining your AI models against the most formidable peers in the field. Whether your focus lies on designing an algorithm to optimize complex logistical networks or delicately crafting a prompt to enhance the subtleties of conversational AI, each challenge is a profound opportunity to push your personal limits and expand your repository of understanding.

A prominent lighthouse in the realm of data science competitions is Kaggle. This platform extends an abundance of opportunities to aspiring data scientists and AI aficionados alike, providing them a veritable playground for engagement with intricate datasets, collaborative endeavors with fellow thinkers, and the sharpening of their machine learning prowess. It's a dynamic space where the blend of theoretical knowledge and practical application comes alive. Meanwhile, another exciting pursuit exists within the confines of OpenAI's challenges, which are specifically tailored to propel the boundaries of prompt engineering into uncharted territory. These competitions are meticulously designed to not only stimulate innovative thinking but also arm participants with the essential tools and resources crucial for success. By embarking on these ventures, you're engaged not just in personal skill enhancement but also actively integrating into a global network, a thriving community that deeply values ingenuity and persistent problem-solving.

To achieve success in these competitive arenas often necessitates a balance between strategic thinking and effective collaboration. Envision assembling a team composed of diverse members, each bringing a unique spectrum of expertise and perspectives, collectively pooling their knowledge towards achieving a common goal. This diversity is not merely beneficial—it is instrumental in fostering an environment that catalyzes creativity and innovation, culminating in more robust, resilient solutions. Delving into the historical successes of past competition winners can be equally enlightening. By deconstructing and understanding the nuances that made their approaches successful, you can tailor and refine your strategies, thereby enhancing and fortifying your chances of success. It is a valuable exercise in learning from the best, perpetually evolving with each new challenge.

The advantages of participating in these challenges transcend far beyond the immediate horizon of skill development. They present profound opportunities to construct a professional portfolio enriched with demonstrations of your capabilities and accomplishments. Picture yourself showcasing your competition experiences and results to prospective employers or clients, evidencing your adeptness at tackling and overcoming complex problems while delivering substantive, tangible results. The mere act of winning or even participating in these challenges can serve as a conduit to open doors otherwise sealed, furnishing networking opportunities that can be pivotal in this competitive domain. The recognition garnered from peers and industry stalwarts can markedly elevate your career trajectory, providing the exposure necessary to thrive and advance in this dynamic field.

Moreover, engaging in AI challenges transcends the boundaries of technical proficiency—it is a transformative experience that cultivates resilience, adaptability, and pioneering innovation. Every competition embarked upon is a fresh chapter in your professional odyssey, replete with prospects for learning, growth, and connectivity with fellow enthusiasts who share your zeal for technology. As you navigate and traverse this exhilarating landscape, always bear in mind that success is not solely epitomized by triumph but rather by the voluminous wealth of acquired knowledge and experiences harvested along the way. These challenges serve as your portal to not simply participating in the realm of AI, but actively contributing to shaping and molding its promising future.

Leveraging Social Media for Learning and Networking

Think of social media as a bustling digital marketplace, teeming with opportunities to connect, learn, and showcase your expertise in the AI field. Platforms like LinkedIn and Twitter have become indispensable tools for professionals eager to carve out a niche in this rapidly evolving landscape. LinkedIn serves as your digital business card, a place where you can build professional connections, seek job opportunities, and engage with industry leaders. It's where you can join AI groups, follow companies spearheading innovation, and participate in discussions that could shape your career. Meanwhile, Twitter is your portal to real-time updates and insights from AI thought leaders. By following hashtags such as #AIResearch and #PromptEngineering, you gain access to a wealth of knowledge and perspectives from across the globe.

Social media's power lies not just in connectivity but in the ability to stay informed. Engaging with AI-focused discussions and webinars on these platforms keeps you on the cutting edge of technology. Imagine scrolling through your feed and stumbling upon a live discussion with leading experts dissecting the latest AI breakthroughs. These interactions are not mere passive consumption; they are active learning experiences that enrich your understanding and broaden your horizons. Participating in these conversations by asking questions or sharing insights builds your reputation as an engaged and informed member of the AI community.

Building a personal brand within the AI sphere is more crucial than ever. Social media offers a stage for you to share original content and insights, positioning yourself as a thought leader. This isn't about self-promotion but about contributing value to a community hungry for knowledge. By consistently posting articles, case studies, or even short reflections on your learning journey, you demonstrate your expertise and commitment to growth. Engage with peers' posts by offering constructive feedback or sharing resources. This reciprocity strengthens your network and solidifies your presence.

Successful social media engagement is not an abstract concept; it's embodied by individuals and organizations effectively using these platforms to amplify their reach and impact. Consider AI influencers who regularly share research findings or innovations, sparking conversations that ripple through the industry. Companies highlight their AI breakthroughs, attracting talent and fostering partnerships through strategic content sharing. Their success stems from authenticity, consistency, and the genuine value they offer to their audience. Observe these examples not as distant aspirations but as tangible models you can emulate in your journey.

To maximize your social media strategy, focus on consistent engagement rather than sporadic bursts of activity. Establish a content calendar that outlines when and what you'll post, ensuring that you maintain a steady presence. Quality trumps quantity; even a single well-thought-out post can have significant impact if it resonates with your audience. Engage with comments on your posts promptly, fostering dialogue and building relationships. Recognize that social media is a two-way street; it's as much about listening as it is about speaking.

When considering which platforms to prioritize, think about where your target audience spends their time. LinkedIn is ideal for professional networking, while Twitter offers quick insights and real-time interactions. Align your efforts with your goals, whether it's expanding your network, enhancing your knowledge, or establishing yourself as an expert. Explore new features like Twitter Spaces or LinkedIn Live to diversify how you connect with others.

As you navigate social media, remain authentic to your voice and perspective. Authenticity builds trust, which is the foundation of any successful brand. Share both successes and challenges, creating a relatable image that invites others to connect with you on a deeper level. Remember that building an online presence takes time; patience and perseverance will yield results.

Social media's role in learning and networking extends beyond the superficial scrolling of feeds; it's about creating meaningful connections and continuously evolving through shared knowledge. Whether you're engaging with a tweet from a renowned researcher or participating in a LinkedIn discussion about AI ethics, each interaction enriches your understanding and expands your network. Seize these opportunities to learn from industry leaders, contribute your insights, and carve out your niche in the vibrant world of AI.

Accessing Support Networks: Mentoring and Peer Groups

Imagine standing at the foot of a daunting mountain, the peak obscured by swirling mist. The climb ahead seems insurmountable, yet a seasoned guide appears beside you, offering wisdom from countless ascents. This is the essence of mentorship—a guiding hand that illuminates the path, transforming the arduous climb into a journey of discovery. In the realm of AI and prompt engineering, mentors and peer groups serve as these invaluable guides, providing not just direction but also motivation and accountability.

Support networks, both formal and informal, are crucial in fostering personal and professional growth. They open doors to diverse perspectives and expertise that would otherwise remain closed. Engaging with mentors and peers allows you to draw from a tapestry of experiences, enriching your understanding and expanding your horizons. Whether it's gaining insights from someone who has navigated similar challenges or exploring fresh ideas during group discussions, these interactions are golden opportunities for learning and growth.

Finding these networks can be as simple as exploring AI mentorship initiatives offered by professional organizations. Many industry bodies are eager to connect budding enthusiasts with seasoned professionals who can provide guidance tailored to your career aspirations. Additionally, platforms like Meetup offer AI study groups where you can connect with peers who share your interests. These gatherings are not just about learning; they're about building a community of like-minded individuals who support each other in their pursuits.

The role of mentors extends far beyond mere knowledge transfer. They can fast-track your learning and career progression by offering tailored advice that aligns with your unique goals. Imagine having someone who provides feedback on your projects, suggests resources, and introduces you to key figures in the industry. A mentor can open doors to networking opportunities that might otherwise remain closed, helping you navigate the complexities of your chosen field with confidence.

But mentorship is not a one-way street; it's a reciprocal relationship where both parties learn and grow. As you gain insights and skills, you contribute fresh perspectives that enrich the mentor's understanding as well. This dynamic exchange fosters a culture of continuous learning and mutual respect, wherein both mentor and mentee benefit from the relationship.

Equally important are peer-led activities that encourage active participation and collaboration. Engaging in peer-led workshops and hackathons offers hands-on experience that deepens your understanding of AI concepts. These events provide a platform for experimentation, allowing you to test ideas in a supportive environment where trial and error are part of the learning process. Collaborative research and project development are other avenues for growth, offering opportunities to work alongside peers on real-world problems that challenge your creativity and analytical skills.

Participation in these activities builds more than technical expertise; it cultivates soft skills such as teamwork, communication, and leadership. These are invaluable assets in any career, equipping you to navigate complex interpersonal dynamics and lead projects effectively. By actively engaging with your peers, you develop a network of contacts who can offer support, feedback, and collaboration opportunities throughout your career.

In this digital age, connecting with mentors and peers has never been easier. Virtual platforms erase geographical barriers, allowing you to engage with experts and enthusiasts from around the globe. Whether through video calls, online forums, or social media groups, these connections provide a wealth of knowledge and support at your fingertips.

To make the most of these networks, approach them with an open mind and a willingness to learn. Be proactive in seeking out mentors whose experiences align with your goals, and participate actively in peer groups where you feel comfortable sharing ideas and feedback. Remember that the value of these networks lies in the relationships you build—relationships founded on trust, respect, and mutual growth.

As you explore these support networks, you'll find they offer more than just guidance; they provide a sense of belonging in a community united by shared passions and aspirations. Through mentorship and peer collaboration, you unlock new possibilities for learning and growth in the ever-evolving world of AI and prompt engineering.

Building a Personal Brand in the AI Community

In the ever-evolving world of AI, where innovation is constant and the pace is relentless, establishing a personal brand is not just an advantage—it is a necessity. When you think of personal branding, envision it as setting your unique signature in a crowded room, a way to distinguish yourself amid the myriad voices and ideas. In a competitive market where everyone is trying to make their mark, your brand becomes your identity, speaking on your behalf even before you enter the conversation. It's the beacon that attracts career opportunities and collaborations, signaling to others what you stand for and what you can offer. By crafting a strong personal brand, you establish credibility and influence, making it easier for potential collaborators and employers to find and recognize your value.

Creating this brand requires deliberate action and consistency. Start by building a professional online presence. This means curating your profiles on key platforms like LinkedIn, ensuring they reflect your interests and achievements in AI. Share insights, experiences, and lessons learned—these become the building blocks of your reputation. Consistently providing valuable content, whether through articles, videos, or blog posts, positions you as an informed voice in the field. It's not about shouting the loudest but about speaking with clarity and purpose. Remember, your online persona should mirror your offline values and expertise. This alignment fosters trust and authenticity.

Thought leadership plays a pivotal role in enhancing your brand. By establishing yourself as a thought leader, you not only share knowledge but also shape discourse in your area of expertise. Publish articles that dive deep into current AI trends or present case studies showcasing successful projects you've tackled. These publications serve as testaments to your expertise and contribute to the broader AI community's knowledge pool. Additionally, speaking at conferences and webinars can elevate your status from participant to influencer. These platforms offer opportunities to connect with others on a large scale, positioning you as a go-to expert in your niche.

Consider those who have successfully leveraged personal branding to become thought leaders in AI. Look at educators like Andrew Ng, whose online courses have reached millions, or researchers like Fei-Fei Li, whose work in computer vision has inspired countless others. These individuals have not only contributed significant advancements to AI but have also built brands synonymous with excellence and innovation (The state of AI in 2023: Generative AI's breakout year). Entrepreneurs in the field often use their personal brands to fuel growth, attracting investment and talent by showcasing their vision and leadership.

In building your brand, focus on what sets you apart. Identify your unique strengths and passions within AI and let these guide your branding efforts. Are you particularly skilled in developing intuitive user interfaces for AI systems? Or do you excel in simplifying complex algorithms for broader audiences? Whatever it is, make it the cornerstone of your branding strategy. This focus differentiates you from others and makes your contributions memorable.

Remember, personal branding is an ongoing process. It requires nurturing and adaptation as both you and the industry evolve. Regularly assess your brand's alignment with your goals and adjust your strategies accordingly. Engage actively with your audience by responding to comments, participating in discussions, and staying updated on industry changes. This engagement not only strengthens your brand but also keeps you connected to the community's pulse.

As we conclude this chapter on personal branding within the AI community, reflect on how these strategies can propel you forward in this dynamic field. Building a personal brand isn't just about self-promotion; it's about creating a legacy that speaks to your contributions and vision within AI. In the next chapter, we'll explore how these principles extend beyond individual branding to influence team dynamics and collaboration within AI-driven projects. Embrace the opportunity to craft a brand that resonates with authenticity and authority, opening doors to new possibilities and connections in the vast landscape of artificial intelligence.

Conclusion

As we reach the end of our journey together, I hope you've found a new appreciation for the vast possibilities that prompt engineering and AI offer. We've navigated through the fundamentals of artificial intelligence, explored the intricate art of crafting prompts, and ventured into real-world applications. From understanding how AI can transform customer service to discovering ways to monetize your newfound skills, you've gathered a toolkit designed to help you work smarter and potentially earn more.

Throughout this book, we've revisited the core principles of AI and prompt engineering, highlighting the importance of clarity and context in crafting effective prompts. You've learned strategies for maintaining consistency and efficiency in your work. We've tackled common challenges and explored how to overcome them with confidence. The potential to enhance your career opportunities and stay ahead in this rapidly evolving field is within your grasp.

Remember, this isn't just about knowledge—it's about application. It's one thing to read about these concepts, but it's an entirely different experience to put them into practice. I encourage you to take the techniques and strategies we've discussed and apply them in your daily life. Experiment with prompts, engage with AI tools, and don't be afraid to make mistakes. Each attempt is a step forward on your path to mastery.

The vision for this book was simple yet powerful: to empower you to master AI tools like ChatGPT and Claude, enabling you to work smarter and earn faster. The skills you've developed here have the potential to transform how you interact with technology, opening up new opportunities for growth and innovation.

Consider this your call to action. Dive into the additional resources provided, join community forums, and explore further education opportunities. The AI landscape is vast and ever-changing, and your journey has just begun. Keep learning, stay curious, and continue to build on the foundation you've established.

As you embark on this exciting journey, remember that challenges are not roadblocks—they are opportunities for growth. Embrace them with confidence. You've got the tools and the knowledge to tackle anything that comes your way.

Reflecting on my own journey, I can relate to the excitement and challenges you may face. My passion for helping beginners in AI stems from my own experiences. I've seen firsthand how these skills can empower individuals and open doors to new possibilities. Sharing this knowledge with you has been a rewarding experience, and I am grateful for the opportunity to be part of your learning journey.

Thank you for your commitment and dedication. Your willingness to learn and explore new horizons is commendable. As you move forward, know that you're not alone. The AI community is supportive and full of like-minded individuals ready to share insights and encourage you along the way.

Looking to the future, the possibilities in AI and prompt engineering are limitless. With your newfound skills and knowledge, you have the power to be a pioneer in this evolving field. Imagine the impact you can make—not just in your career, but in shaping the future of technology.

Go forth with confidence, curiosity, and a sense of adventure. The world of AI awaits, and I am excited to see where this journey takes you. Here's to a future filled with innovation, growth, and success.

References

- *Prompt Engineering Guide: The Ultimate ...* https://learnprompting.org/docs/introduction?srsltid=AfmBOop-ACNJjfGBs_xVevMYemE2fKs6p-qTETxR3IM42zH3r4y2z6BD
- *Natural Language Processing Key Terms, Explained* https://www.kdnuggets.com/2017/02/natural-language-processing-key-terms-explained.html
- *How LLMs Like ChatGPT and Claude Actually Works?* https://medium.com/@seekmeai/how-llms-like-chatgpt-and-claude-actually-works-859f076025d0
- *Debunking 10 Misconceptions About AI* https://365datascience.com/trending/debunking-misconceptions-ai/
- *The ultimate guide to writing effective AI prompts* https://www.atlassian.com/blog/artificial-intelligence/ultimate-guide-writing-ai-prompts
- *The Importance of Context: Crafting Effective Prompts for ...* https://www.linkedin.com/pulse/importance-context-crafting-effective-prompts-better-prasad-mba-phd-lh7tc#:~:text=The%20more%20context%20you%20provide,accurate%2C%20engaging%2C%20and%20useful.
- *Beyond "Prompt and Pray": 14 Prompt Engineering Mistakes ...* https://odsc.medium.com/beyond-prompt-and-pray-14-prompt-engineering-mistakes-youre-probably-still-making-c2c3a32711bc
- *Prompt Engineering: A Practical Example* https://realpython.com/practical-prompt-engineering/
- *How does AI improve customer service and contact center ...* https://www.talkdesk.com/blog/how-does-ai-improve-customer-service-and-contact-

center-efficiency/

- *Case Studies on Successful AI-Driven Marketing Campaigns* https://www.markopolo.ai/post/case-studies-on-successful-ai-driven-marketing-campaigns
- *How to become a freelance AI prompt engineer - IPSE* https://www.ipse.co.uk/advice/how-to-become-a-freelance-ai-prompt-engineer
- *CROSS-INDUSTRY INNOVATION: HOW AI IS ...* https://medium.com/@tiffany-cheong/cross-industry-innovation-how-ai-is-facilitating-unlikely-collaborations-301f6a3dcc32
- *How to Generate Brand-Consistent Content with AI* https://www.copy.ai/guides/how-to-generate-brand-consistent-content-with-ai
- *Top 5 Prompt Engineering Tools for Evaluating Prompts* https://blog.promptlayer.com/top-5-prompt-engineering-tools-for-evaluating-prompts/
- *Prompt Engineering: creating effective AI prompts (ChatGPT ...* https://nation.ai/prompt-engineering-how-to-formulate-effective-prompts-to-master-generative-ai-chatgpt-claude-gemini/
- *Balancing Creativity and Constraints in AI Prompt Design* https://qurtoo.com/balancing-creativity-and-constraints-in-ai-prompt-design/
- *Understanding AI: Overcoming Fear And Embracing The ...* https://elearningindustry.com/understanding-ai-overcoming-fear-and-embracing-the-future
- *8 Time Management Tips for Students - Harvard Summer School* https://summer.harvard.edu/blog/8-time-management-tips-for-students/
- *AI for Everyone: Building an AI Education Ecosystem with ...* https://www.aspeninstitute.org/blog-posts/ai-for-everyone-building-an-ai-education-ecosystem-with-community-colleges-across-america/
- *Case Studies: Successful Applications of Prompt Engineering* https://medium.com/@devlexus/case-studies-successful-applications-of-prompt-engineering-4984a161101b
- *Exploring the Prospects of Prompt Engineering as a Career ...* https://medium.com/all-things-work/exploring-the-prospects-of-prompt-engineering-as-a-career-path-95f0a906373d
- *Success Stories in Prompt Engineering Case Studies* https://moldstud.com/a

rticles/p-success-stories-in-prompt-engineering-case-studies
- *Effective AI Networking Strategies for Mid-Career ...* https://www.linkedin.com/advice/3/heres-how-you-can-network-build-connections-pcekf
- *Learn Prompting: Your Guide to Communicating with AI* https://learnprompting.org/?srsltid=AfmBOopsaREKfvAxFXRd9uAhB4pUbcvPu5FIQJZLQ-5hTI9iLUlJf7nD
- *The state of AI in 2023: Generative AI's breakout year* https://www.mckinsey.com/capabilities/quantumblack/our-insights/the-state-of-ai-in-2023-generative-ais-breakout-year
- *Artificial intelligence | MIT News | Massachusetts Institute of ...* https://news.mit.edu/topic/artificial-intelligence2
- *The Ultimate List: Top 100 AI Tools in 2023 (Updated August)* http://medium.com/design-bootcamp/the-ultimate-list-top-100-ai-tools-in-2023-65c5ea1ccbd9
- *The Future of Prompt Engineering: Trends to Watch in 2025* https://aigptjournal.com/explore-ai/ai-prompts/prompt-engineering-trends-2025/
- *Top AI Communities in 2023 - Medium* https://medium.com/ai-vanguard/top-ai-communities-in-2023-403254cb05f1
- *15 of the Best AI Competitions in 2024* https://www.inspiritai.com/blogs/ai-blog/ai-competition
- *Best social media platform for Ai-interested audience* https://www.reddit.com/r/SocialMediaMarketing/comments/1jcn9fc/best_social_media_platform_for_aiinterested/
- *Research Mentorship Program in Artificial Intelligence* https://www.inspiritai.com/blogs/ai-student-blog/research-mentorship-program-in-ai

www.ingramcontent.com/pod-product-compliance
Lightning Source LLC
LaVergne TN
LVHW051051210926
848486LV00002B/70